THE
Lost Art of Loving

Johanna Carroll

The Lost Art of Loving
by: Johanna Carroll

Published by
Christine F. Anderson Publishing & Media, Madison VA, 22727
www.publishwithcfa.com

CHRISTINE F. ANDERSON
PUBLISHING & MEDIA

ISBN: 978-0692640647

Printed in the United States of America

I dedicate this book to all seekers of love and good heart health. To all my amazing clients over the last thirty years I thank you for your stories. I consider all of you my spiritual children and am blessed to have you in my life. I always wanted a daughter and now I have thousands of them! I also want to thank my spiritual male clients as well for giving me the male moments in this book. You are all amazing souls and I dedicate this to your continued growth and evolution. You are each a precious pearl in my life.

To my sons Scot and David who still think I'm a cool Mom. I dedicate this also to my wonderful Divine Complement and husband Floyd. Thank you for not doing laundry during my writing hours and keeping the cat quiet. I also appreciate the meals every night, a clean house and all the grocery shopping. You were my amazing nurse when I was recuperating from my heart surgeries and you continue to support me all the time. I thank and bless you a million times for your unconditional love and devotion to our marriage.

Table of Contents

Part IV: Loving in the New Age

Part V: Seasons of Love

Epilogue

Introduction
The Story of My Life

I am proud to be a scribe for the Universe. My clients refer to me as their spiritual mom, mentor and some call me spiritual sister or auntie. Throughout the ages many sages and ascended masters have taught that all we feel think or do has a direct impact on our physical well being. This is often referred to as the body mind and spirit connection. A significant health scare reminded me I was not infallible. The words that I wish to share with you were always heard and felt during deep meditations and then written down.

These words came across the veils of time like a whisper from eternity and spilled across a page like a strand of precious pearls. The story of my health scare around my heart is what birthed this loving book.

It all began with the need for two emergency heart surgeries within two weeks of each other. I had originally gone to my primary care doctor six months prior to these surgeries. I told him I had shortness of breath, a pressure on my chest, cold sweats, dizziness, very poor sleep at night and was sometimes nauseous. After eight to nine hours of sleep at night, I woke up totally exhausted. At the end of the day, I felt as if anyone touched me gently with a finger push, I would just fall over. I am not sure anyone really believed how exhausted I was.

My primary care doctor was concerned and sent me to a cardiologist and suggested I 'may' need a stress test. I saw this cardiologist three times within a six month period, always with the same symptoms. I did not have all of those symptoms each time I saw him, and I asked if I should have a stress test each time and was told no. I was sent to a sleep disorder center for evaluation for breathing and oxygenation tests. The physician's assistant informed me they were going to put me on at-home equipment testing for sleep apnea.

The physician's assistant I worked with in the sleep center was certain I had sleep apnea and the tests confirmed that I did. I was then given a CPAP machine to wear at night and was told all my exhaustion and sleep problems would go away. They did not go away. I tried to get used to the machine but struggled with it over a few weeks time.

Six months after I had continually requested a stress test from my doctor, I found myself in a Silver Sneakers (senior citizen) aerobics class fainting. Initially I thought I had not eaten enough breakfast. I grabbed my water bottle and sat down for a few minutes because I could not breathe. Subsequently, later that day, I went out to get our mail. We have a very long driveway and after grabbing the mail, I didn't think I was going to make it back to the house. I imagined myself crawling down the driveway but instead walked very slowly back into the house. As soon as I got in, I called my cardiologist's office and said that I needed to see him ASAP. I was told that he could see me in five weeks. My response was I can not wait that long. I explained to the nurse I had just gone onto the Internet to check heart symptoms for women and I had all of them. She magically found me an appointment the next day.

Here is some information I found on the Internet under American Heart Association for heart attack symptoms in women. The old adage that you have to have a searing abrupt pain in your chest and your left arm going numb is not a one size fits all for men and women.

CAUSES OF A HEART ATTACK IN WOMEN

Heart disease is the No. 1 killer of women, which is why it is imperative that women learn the warning signs and symptoms, see a doctor regularly, and learn their family history.

SYMPTOMS OF A HEART ATTACK:

- Uncomfortable pressure, squeezing, fullness or pain in the center of your chest that lasts more than a few minutes, or goes away and comes back.

- Pain or discomfort in one or both arms, the back, neck, jaw or stomach.

- Shortness of breath, with or without chest discomfort.

- Other signs such as breaking out in a cold sweat, nausea or lightheadedness.

As with men, the most common heart attack symptom in women is chest pain or discomfort. But it's important to note that women are more likely to experience the other common symptoms, particularly shortness of breath, nausea/vomiting and back or jaw pain.

WHAT TO DO DURING A HEART ATTACK

If you experience any of these signs or symptoms:

- Do not wait to call for help. Dial 9-1-1, make sure to follow the operator's instructions and get to a hospital right away.

- Do not drive yourself or have someone drive you to the hospital unless you have no other choice.

- Try to stay as calm as possible and take deep, slow breaths while you wait for the emergency responders.

WHY IT'S IMPORTANT TO KNOW THE SYMPTOMS OF A HEART ATTACK

Women who consider themselves healthy often misdiagnose the symptoms of a heart attack because they don't think it could happen to them. That is why it's crucial to learn about heart disease and stroke, know your numbers, live a heart-healthy lifestyle and be aware of the risk factors of heart disease.

I don't know why but it is my belief that most women ignore pain. Maybe it is from having babies which my mother in law referred to as walking throughout the Valley of Death. I think we suck it up and pray it will go away so we can continue with that huge to do list we all have embedded in our brains. Have we forgotten what it feels like to be healthy? Have we accepted that feeling 'off' is the norm? I still get mad at myself for thinking oh this too shall pass. At this point I implore you if you have any of the symptoms listed above to put this book down and call your doctor immediately. Do not ignore your body when it is trying to tell you something.

My chest pressure had accelerated over six months into a tight feeling around my chest—like my bra was too tight or someone was wrapping elastic bands around my body. I had reported this to my cardiologist three times in six months of office visits. Each time he told me my heart was fine. I decided during this next visit to demand a stress test.

So when I went to see him I told him, "Look I need a stress test. I am having chest pain along with everything else. You do realize that female symptoms are different from men, right Doctor?" Now I had his attention. "Well, I don't like the chest pain, he said, let's schedule a stress test." I gritted my teeth and held back what I really wanted to say.

I went for the stress test two days later, still feeling like crap, and failed it miserably.

They started with a nuclear isotope injection in my arm which was followed up with a radiology scan. I had to go to the building next door for the actual treadmill stress test.

There was a little elevation to the sidewalk, and as I walked to the next building, pulling the gorgeous blue printed hospital gown around me, I had to stop three times because I could not breathe. As everyone rushed by me I thought I hope I don't drop dead on this sidewalk in this horrible hospital gown. Slowly I made it to the building and the department where I started the next round of tests. I told the nurse, "You know I don't feel so great so please take it easy on me." The nurse told me that she had to get my heart rate up to a rate that I could hold for at least five minutes to get a true reading. "OK", I said, "I will try the best I can."

The treadmill is set on an incline, and I was doubtful I could even do it. Although I had been playing tennis for a long time, I did not do well on inclines. In fact, while on a vacation in Mexico two months prior, I could hardly walk through the sand and attributed that to my fitness level. I remember my husband saying, "You know maybe you should go to the gym a little bit more." As soon as I got halfway through the treadmill test, and I said that my chest was burning, which for me means pain; they took me off, laid me down on a bed, put nitroglycerin under my tongue and gave me oxygen. They called in the doctor on site, and he told me that I had failed the test badly and there was a major problem. I said, "Really, are you sure?" His response was that if I were his wife or mother, I would not leave this hospital. I needed surgery. He said, "Here are your choices: surgery or heart attack."

The nurses got a hold of the cardiologist I was seeing at the time. He came in, looked at the test results and said, "Wow, I am so glad I ordered this stress test." I wanted to slap him. He told me I needed to go down to surgery for an angiogram to see what was going on in my heart. After the doctor left the stress test room three nurses stood before me. One was holding my hand, another was hugging me because I started to cry. I told them that I was scared. They all told me the same thing: Thank God you got the stress test because we see so many women who wait too long. They either show up here after having a massive heart attack or even worse come in dead. I told them my story about asking for a stress test for over six months and being told I didn't need one. They all looked at each other and said the same thing, listen to your body you know when something is wrong.

The surgeon met me in the prep room and explained the procedure. He also told me that while he was in there, if anything needed to be done, he would do it. Then he asked me my history. After I told him about my six months of being ignored he told me heard this all the time. "Doctor, you need to go back and tell your buddies to pay attention to women when they come in with complaints. We are not a bunch of hysterical hypochondriacs!"

I had starting praying for the Universe to protect me the moment I was told I needed surgery. They protected me so well no one could even get a needle into my arm to deliver medication. I had eight needle holes in my arms and was about to start surgery without drugs. They decided to deliver the sedatives through my groin area and I was told, "Hold on, you will feel like an elephant is stilling on you." They were right on that one!

My husband and son were in shock when the surgeon told them an hour later that I had two fully blocked arteries and he needed to insert stents into them. He also told them I had too much dye in my system, and I had to come back in two weeks for the other artery. He was concerned that excessive dye would shut down my kidneys. The first surgery was a little over an hour; the second one was over three hours as it was more complicated.

Once again I am so protected by the Universe. One of my arteries that was blocked had started to grow a new set of smaller arteries at the end, like volunteers grow from plants. This was the only source of blood to my heart. Again, after hearing about this, I felt a miracle was created to keep me alive. I am now fully recovered; I fired the first cardiologist for obvious reasons and am very happy with my new doctor. I did go back to my primary care doctor to report back in with him. I told him what happened and this is what he said, "We screw up and we make mistakes." No apology, no I am sorry. Just we screw up. "Doctor, I could have died; I was a walking heart attack." He just nodded and said nothing. Doctors are not gods and they don't have all the answers, but a little compassion would have gone a long way. I was blessed to have one of the best heart surgeons in the country who is also a scientist and a brilliant man. I would like to say I was lucky he was there but I think I really to thank the Universe and divine timing.

Prologue

any people consider me a mouthpiece for the divine. Now I had to be my own spiritual counselor to figure out why my heart was ready to give up. Did my emotional adjustment to a new marriage affect my heart health? Did the rejection of my birth family all those years ago do physical injury to my heart besides my soul? I am a seeker on a spiritual path seeking more wisdom just like you. There is always more to learn. What did I need to do differently to understand the healing of my heart? It was time for a review once again. Wouldn't you look at your life and seek the something that made your heart go boom boom boom? Wouldn't you want to know how love and relationships needed to be seen with a fresh set of eyes? How many times had I suggested to my clients to put on their spiritual glasses and see life differently. Did I need a new spiritual prescription to see my life anew? If relationships were really the cause of my heart failing me, where did I fail my heart? How could I do it better in my second chance to heal love?

I sat in my office one hot sunny morning wrapped in my red pashmina prayer shawl. I was just coming out of a meditation and had my normal silent dialogue with the divine.

"Ok you guys it wasn't my time and I wasn't supposed to cross over—which I could have easily done. I would like to know what I need to do spiritually to improve not only my physical health but my emotional health as well. Show me the way please" I quietly prayed. That is when I clearly heard the words The Lost Art of Loving. "Is this a book," I asked out loud? A green light flashes behind my closed eyes which for me is a clear sign meaning yes. It was time to get back to work get some awareness and create some magic.

Throughout this book you will find terminology that is related to timeless spiritual teachings often called Universal truths. They have been found in the Sanskrit and Pali languages, the Vedic teachings of the Bhagavad Gita and the Upanishads to name a few. These eternal truths and terms are also integrated into the later works of Emerson, Melville and Thoreau. We see these referred to in every age. They belong to humanity and therefore to you. What matters most is that these teachings help you deal with your life and resonate with your soul.

PART 1

THE ESSENCE OF LOVE

Love is Wholeness

Everyone has a different perception of happiness. We crave love. Have we forgotten how to love? Can we give and receive love that will fill our heart like a cup overflowing with joy, bliss and happiness? Is love so illusive it falls like the coarse sands of time between our fingers? Are we running out of time for love? Have we given up? It's almost too much to process and therein lays the challenge. We spend so much time analyzing love and trying to figure out love that we forget what we already know: we are love.

Really? What the heck does that mean? I am love. If I am love, Universe, then prove it to me. Show me show me show me. Give me one of your mystical signs. I don't need a flaming arrow into my heart to know its there. If I am love, then why do I sometimes feel sad? When will that full cup of yummy love be more than a temporary visitor in my life? Am I missing something here? What do I need to do differently?

I chose not to go home to heaven; I am still here. I even surrendered and said I would go but no, you said, "Not your time, sister. You have more work to do. Can you give me a few pearls of wisdom, a little advice on a shortcut to happiness?"

I sat and waited and of course got the answer I didn't necessarily want to hear. "Shortcut, are you kidding me? Your soul has been around the block like a million times and now you want a shortcut?"

I agree, I have been around the block a million times and multiple lifetimes. I had been so tired I felt like I could just lay down and die and I almost did!

"At least I'm asking. It's not just for me. I have a lot of souls to help here so lighten up."

In my moments of curious contemplation my soul knew what the lost art of genuine loving was. We all want to be loved whether it is an intimate relationship, family or 13

friends. The quest of a true open heart is simple: we just want to be happy. We look to find happiness always yearning for something more, something better. Don't let the world of advertising define your happiness.

I have profound respect for those who have done the inner work, taken time to ponder once again, how to love, who to love and what to do differently to find genuine peace and happiness. 'I just give up' is a common statement. It appears it is such a quandary for all of us. I believe that for everyone, we want to know love in a way that is almost foreign to us. It is like a journey to a new land, a time we remember and can't quite forget yet it is out of our reach. Illusive. We may even take this journey alone, without anyone by our side, and are perfectly fine. Yet we seek the ultimate sense of love dwelling within as part of our daily life. There is a desire to feel whole and complete. We want this. We want that loving feeling like the song says. Our soul calls to the memory of being wrapped in warmth, peace, joy and bliss. We remember the wholeness of love as part of our divine inheritance.

Love is a state of being. It is a noun, not a verb. It has absolutely nothing to do with someone else. It is a field of vibration, a house in heaven, a dimension in the Universe.

It doesn't matter what label works for you, pick one that feels right. It is not beyond you, it is all around you and inside of you. It is the divine essence from which your soul makes a decision to return to the body and experience life once again. This physical body you exist in has an inner sacred temple. Within this temple are jewels and pearls of wisdom that adorn your heart. Similarly a deep precious love is there just waiting to be experienced. What you see in the mirror is a reflection of the outer person. What you feel within is the soul call to deeper love.

For thirty years my psychic eyes have seen a field of circulating light that surrounds the human body. It is filled with color, sound, movement, taste, and has a feeling as it moves and swirls all around the physical body. In sacred teachings it is referred to as the astral body or Over-Soul. It plays a huge role in returning you to remembering the lost art of loving. It is a magnetic field of memory. It is alive with divine intention to return you home to the state of divine wholeness.

Love is. It merely is. It is the most powerful force that allows us to feel the presence of eternal intelligence that lives in every crazy cell of our being. It holds us together. Love pours the soul into the body. Consider it the glue of the Universe. The scotch tape of heaven. The Velcro of the cosmos we know is there but do not see. Love is the bonding agent that gives us life, continues with us in all realms and never abandons us. We abandon Love.

One of the secrets I learned through activating the higher teachings around the lost art of loving was connecting with this astral body and what I could actually do with it. I could mold something. I could bend light and I could manifest anything. I could define my destiny. I could peek into the heavens. I could ask a question and get an answer. I was on board pulling the threads of the astral body and creating something out of nothing. I was weaving a garment of wisdom. I didn't have to sit around waiting for the bang over the head. I had a choice to become an active co-partner with the Universe. When love is used it creates upon itself, it creates more love. A larger bottle of glue that is endless.

The Universe and I were partners in creating something pretty amazing. I had a second chance to review and renew my life. I welcomed a return to the wholeness of love to heal everything.

Intelligence comes as a result of living a life and gathering knowledge. Gathering the knowledge through your life experiences is not enough. You may be smart but that doesn't make you wise. It's like riding a merry-go-round in the park, repeat repeat repeat the same old lessons before the soul can gather that precious pearl of wisdom.

Knowledge that is applied transcends the human condition and becomes realized wisdom. Knowledge that says, uh oh, this feels familiar but I need to do it differently is soul evolution. You grow as a person through knowledge and your soul evolves. This is the game plan of the soul. Smart as a person, wise as a soul. It is a partnership of humanity and divinity walking hand in hand through life with confidence that something far greater is guiding the journey. Wisdom that is divinely guided is intelligence applied by embracing a change. Miraculously, life changes through your application of wisdom.

You gather another pearl. Bam, lesson learned wisdom gained and no more need to suffer. What a concept.

When love as a state of being is shared, the noun now becomes the verb. It has movement that we share. The state of being love is our own awareness that we are so much more than the body held together by scotch tape. We have aligned our self and soul into one larger entity. We have to acknowledge this is generated first by filling up our own cup, our heart, the pillow for your soul. This is the divine spark that activates the movement so love as an action can be received by something or someone outside of us. It is a flow that delivers the state of being whole into a river of light that activates the feeling of love. We intuitively feel a shift within and without because we have connected to something far greater and wiser than our limited human self. We ignite the divine partnership of self and soul working as one committed entity to living a life with far greater joy than felt before. The feeling of being alone no longer exists because you have all of heaven walking beside you.

The challenge of the sharing of love is questioning whether it is genuine and are we directing it to the 'right' person, place, idea, or situation. That is the biggie. Is this real love? How do you know? The state of love creates a connection from your heart reaching out to deliver and receive love in return. I asked the Universe to give me another pearl of wisdom I could use for myself and share with you. Here is what I heard loud and clear.

"We will remind you of what your soul already knows. Loving is a selfless act." The biggest quest of all time to return to the lost art of loving fully requires this of you; know this is sacred.

Love as a Form of Art

How would love be a form of art? We know we can go to a museum or even go online to look at the masterpieces of the world. Actually going to a museum is an entirely different experience because you are standing before the real deal. If you are wise and open as I know you all are, you connect to it. The art activates a response on a sensory level.

You may see or feel hidden meanings and messages. It speaks to you. The experience becomes more personal and profound. Your heart is touched, a trigger of light goes ping on your soul. You take a deeper breath. You see light coming from the canvas touching your heart. This is definitely a bigger experience and so different than looking at an image on the computer or in a magazine. It personally touches and inspires you to remember the heart and soul of the artist.

You would have missed a great opportunity to feel something beautiful if you had rushed through the art gallery and not paid attention You could have lost a moment in time that may have changed your life. Many human beings fear change. Fear layers the picture of our life with uncertainty and fear. It clouds your vision. Wouldn't you rather see your life as a masterpiece of divinity rather than a fake version created by fear? Where is the original painted by the hands of your soul? In the discovery of your state of being whole you begin to see your life with faith and become fearless. Like a great artisan who is waiting to be discovered, you acknowledge that you are already a master. You call the power of all that love is in every breath, activating each moment merely by stating 'the time is now'. No more wanting no more wishing no more waiting for contentment and bliss. You stand before a painting of yourself in the art gallery of the Universe. This time you feel the emanation of love streaming from every single cell and particle of DNA within. You become the miraculous artistic expression of all the love that ever was. You have discovered what you thought was lost; yourself. You are illuminated.

How We Love

I realized sitting quietly on my patio after my surgeries that I had to really walk my talk.

I wanted good health in my body mind and spirit. I had to completely spiritualize my life with love at every single level. Something magical starts to happen when you spiritualize your life. The roadblocks of sadness and disappointment start to disappear. I needed to remember what I had taught others about how to love. I decided it was important to review the teachings I had created and put them into practice on how to love fearlessly.

"I can't handle the stress anymore" I hear through my telephone while speaking to clients. "I am really struggling about how can I get out of the hole I am in." You didn't watch while someone dug the hole for you. Your hand was on the shovel too. The good news is if you can step back even one tiny little step and reach your hand to the heavens and say "help me" the energy shifts. Challenges may come in many forms. Emotional worries are very hard to control. How to maneuver your life through stressful times almost appears to be impossible. If you can take that one breath, raise your head or hand even if you are lying in bed, if you genuinely call on this source of divine love you will connect. Allow healing to take place. Review how you expect love to serve you and see where you can serve love. Then take a look at how you love.

I believe you understand the concept of conditional and non-conditional love. Just in case you need a little nudge, let me remind you of what your soul already knows. Conditional love is not divine love because it is generated by fear lack and limitations. It is love that has conditions. It is called love but seriously there is no way that this is love in any way shape or form. It is not given freely for the sake of pure love. It is not love that is divinely intended or guided because you cannot barter love as a pure source of soul wholeness.

Conditional love is asking for something in return which generally is some kind of emotional fulfillment we feel we cannot get ourselves. Consider that conditional love creates an environment where there is a push pull type of negotiation. It doesn't work and creates more suffering. This is not genuine love.

We actually practice conditional love with ourselves all the time until we reach that hand up for divine intervention. " If I were thinner, if I were younger, if I were smarter, if I were sexier, if I had more money, if I lived there rather than here," the list of ifs goes on and on. Do you have inner list of ifs? Take a moment close your eyes and be honest with yourself. That is the first step. The first set of conditions you set are limitations on your ability to connect and serve your soul. Remember whatever you believe you are, even unconsciously, you project on to others. I think therefore I am. This would include the people you work with your peers family extended family and most of all your spiritual family in the heart of the heavens. The end result is doubt all the way through the dance of life. This is an exhausting and complicated dance you have chosen. Aren't you tired of this? When you judge you set conditions on how you truly love yourself. If you set this condition of judgment, you are in a lower field of fear based energy that can cause depression mental burn out and health problems. It can give you digestive problems headaches pain exhaustion both mentally and physically. It can create a slower simmer of continual heartache. Sound familiar? If you really want to love yourself, stop the conditional if list.

Unconditional love sounds pretty simple: love without conditions. I love myself for the sake of my soul. I accept myself in the reality of today. Unconditional love exists in the realm of pure love of self, a connection to the divine that dwells within. Therein dwells the inner lover, the higher self of the soul that does not judge. This love merely accepts.

Love that is shared merely for the sake of loving comes without conditions and naturally.

Eternal love embraces all souls all life. No fear or evil can co-exist in a true field of Universal love. Universal love is eternal love. Unconditional love generates compassion understanding and a greater awareness of self. This is the state of love where change serves you. The mental if list is replaced with the I am love list.

The theory of loving yourself from a spiritual point of view when applied purely creates your own life of divine love. Divine love is the magnet that attracts all blessings. It is activated by your intention to be the best you can be without comparing yourself to anyone or anything. Nothing is missing, the spiritual glasses are on and life starts to look pretty darn good. You are sleeping better, eating consciously and not stuffing yourself emotionally on any level with the bread of denial.

The greatest desire of the soul is to share love or our state of divine wholeness. I feel it would be of great value for you to review whether you are operating from a point of conditional or unconditional love. We all want to be loved for who we are without limitations. In the magnetics of the soul we attract what we are. Are you truly reflecting out to the world of relationships a person who will love freely for the sake of love or are you reflecting the message that I am available for love but here are my rules? It is not easy to let go of old beliefs. I would offer that you review what you have been manifesting. If you are content with your choices and results, then I applaud you. If not, what are your conditions for love? Where are you limiting or restricting yourself or others with your needs? Can you let go of the need for approval so you can love freely and be loved merely for the vibrant soul and person you are right now? Can you do this with someone else? Conditional love is where drama lives and it is draining and restrains evolution. How can you merge more gracefully into the arms of love by loving yourself and others unconditionally? It is definitely something to ponder.

How to Manifest Love

*Y*ou cannot be in your head to fully manifest the desires of the soul. You will not get a clear signal from the Over-Soul if the rivers of your life are muddied with the obstacles of confusion. You can clear the confusion by applying the first Law of Manifestation which is clarity. You cannot be clear in your intention in manifesting if you are focusing on the bills your job or anything that is attached to the chaos in your mind. The soul must come first leading the way. How do you do that? Be still and know thyself. Sound familiar?

You do have the ability to call in or manifest love. That loving feeling is available as a continual state of balance and inner peace. What if you truly are ready to share love with another or heal what you have? Then it's time to add to your intention of sharing love and practicing the lost art of loving. When we meditate, we are in the heart and soul of our inner Universe. When we meditate, we are in the divine feminine energy of the Universe.

This means you are nurturing yourself and are allowing yourself to feel the connection to your own unique heart and soul without saying a word. If you can only practice this for five minutes a day, then do it. Try to add to that time where you detach from the outer world and welcome the presence of divinity in your life each day. You have literally plugged into the heart of the Universe by doing this and are now ready to co-create.

We must remember that all activity at some level is food for the ego. We live in an era of information overload so how do you expect to sit quiet at the end of the day to pray or meditate and quiet your mind? You must first release the noise that is in your head so that the head and the heart can be congruent. There is a process called an active meditation that releases the process of all the thoughts in your head that you collect on a daily basis.

You can trick the mind into slowing down and getting rid of the TMI that rolls around in your head daily by doing something active first. Exercise is a great release of mental tension. Hum sing laugh cry or yell and use your voice to start the movement towards inner stillness. Let your body move as you do this. Put on some music and dance around the room. Move your body. Run in your backyard or around a track. Move. Shake away all that extra energy that is in your nervous system. Music at the end of the day is great way to enter the gateway of inner silence. When you feel you are ready, sit down and be still with the music. Your body may be a little restless but resist the urge to get up.

Just sit and listen to the music. Imagine that you are floating on each note and all that matters is the connection you have to this sound. Be still with the music, listen with your heart and see the color of the notes as they float and dissipate. Follow the sound. Imagine a leaf floating on a gentle flowing river. Now be still with your body. As you float on the river of light imagine you are out of your body just watching the river and seeing the water rippling and flowing.

Every single thought feeling word or action that you have or do is a direct instruction to the Universe to create something in your physical world. You are an amazing instrument of energy and along with that energy have power beyond your imagination. Remember I think therefore I am? Your thoughts create people, opportunities, challenges and experiences of all kinds. Instead of letting the world control you, now you get to control your own outer world by paying attention to what you are telling the Universe you want to manifest in love. If you go around telling the Universe 'I am a failure and no one loves me' or 'I will never get the right job' that just might be what you create. That attitude of the victim will get you nowhere other than more suffering. It is a choice.

How would you feel if you woke up and felt happy every day? Make your prayer simple,

"I am continually happy." Try not to attach anyone or anything to that prayer. Get clarity of intention on why you are asking for someone or something. Perhaps you want a healthier body? Maybe its just because you want someone at work to be nicer to you, or you want to heal a misunderstanding with a friend. Go to the feeling first and get clarity on that emotional connection to your soul first. Without doing this, you are only going around the merry go round of your life again and again, repeating those old habits or patterns of behavior that do not serve you in any way at all. Be still. Find the song of your soul, awaken the feeling of being connected to your divine self, and start to feel from the inner heart that is sacred.

We have free will. It is actually a gift from the world of spirit. In your divine plan, there are absolutes or part of your divine destiny and also probabilities and potential.

Absolutes are things that are going to happen no matter what. Some people call this fate.

You are fated to be born and you are fated to die. The gift of life also allows you to direct the traffic of your own life through your choices and free will. You are not fated to make mistakes. Clarity of intention is everything!

You can manifest a life that you could never imagine when you shift your soul intentions.

Instead of giving up, you begin to really see that you are the captain of your own ship.

The destination of the future is part of your free will choices. In order for the ship to sail smoothly, however, its time to pay attention to your old habits around making choices that need to go into the dumpster and stay there. When you ask the Universe to help you with a relationship, besides being clear make sure it is turned over to divine will. Thy will be done. This is another rather simple but powerful teaching. In other words, if this is not for my best and highest good, then bang me on the head let me wake up and move on.

I have had people say to me "you know I think I make terrible choices because all I manifest are mistakes". Please don't beat yourself up if you feel you have made poor choices in the past because you can change that. A psychologist once told me it's not about poor choices. It just means your picker is broken and needs to be fixed. Based on the doozy of relationships I picked before I met my second husband, I would totally agree. It is all about learning discernment.

In the game of divine soul awareness, if you turn your choices over to divine this is a healthy choice. If you again and again feel that your choices in love have failed you, where have you failed your ability to discern a better way? Do you feel you have made poor choices? You are not trapped by your past. There is a blessing in everything including the not so fun experiences that finally did bring you down on your knees asking for help. The blessing is pretty simple. It is wisdom. You have an opportunity to evolve.

The need to learn again and again disappears when you stop repeating old habits. Being smart and using your head is a good start. Applying what you have learned from the past and doing it differently allows the heart to be healed. New choices are birthed from the wisdom of the soul and a profound opportunity to be whole in love is gently placed in your hands.

Where there is love, there is life.

—Gandhi

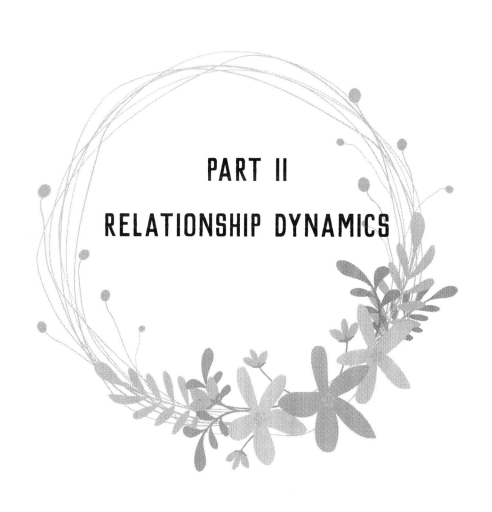

PART II
RELATIONSHIP DYNAMICS

Self-Love

*I*f you are applying the formula of reality, practicality and spirituality, you have to look in the mirror of your soul and do some investigation. You will not at any level activate the magnetics of unconditional love nor return to the lost art of loving unless you begin telling yourself every single thing you love about yourself. Not about your life, not about your possessions but about you as a person. Stop programming your mind with negativity and fall in love with all your imperfections and walk in front of your own parade.

It's an old saying which I feel it is true. You can only love another to the level you love yourself. If someone else's opinion of you is more important than your opinion of yourself, you are not living in the present moment of total awareness. You are nowhere near knowing what it feels like to court your own soul. Are you kind to yourself? Do you judge yourself constantly telling yourself what is wrong? Do you wish you could be someone else? If you wish to wipe the beauty of your soul off the face of the earth keep doing this. You have a choice to retrain your brain and discover the wisdom and joy of self-love.

I challenge you each night before you go to sleep to stand in front of your mirror where you brush your teeth and state out loud three things you love about yourself. Of course you will probably say, "Well I have very nice hair or my eyes are piercing." It's a start.

Then close your eyes and get quiet. Breathe. Up and down in and out just breathe.

Without opening your eyes, silently tell your heart what you love about you. "I was kind today to someone who annoys me. Instead of rushing out of the office, I made an effort to smile and say goodnight to at least two people. I really listened today instead of interrupting thinking what I had to say was more important. I called a friend just to say hello and ask them how they are for no reason at all." Now keep your eyes closed and see what that feels like. Keep breathing. Start the process to open the door to your heart in a way that only expands. Do this each day for a month and after 30 days, check in with your head and your heart. Keep it going by creating a spiritual journal of thoughts that are positive not negative. Be kind be honest and be realistic. Create the I AM IT HIT LIST and start writing, not from your ego but from your soul.

There is another aspect of self-love that many people forget and somehow muddle through. It's called speaking your truth without cutting off some one's head! One of my favorite sayings is it's all in the delivery system. How do you deliver love to yourself in what you say about yourself to others? Be honest with yourself on what works for you and what doesn't work for you. If you aren't truthful in the inner self talk, you will be false with others. What you project you create. Have you ever had someone say to you,

"The problem with you is"? You grit your teeth and wait for the sucker punch right in the gut. Wouldn't it be wonderful if your retort could be, "Thanks for your opinion and here is what I love about myself." There is a falling away of negative opinions when you let go of your negative opinions of yourself. Stop judging yourself. It is no longer attractive to your soul to be a victim.

Speaking your truth from a spiritual place is firm but never harsh or mean. Sometimes we need to clean our spiritual closet and throw away what doesn't fit. This includes the old you who held you back. It also includes people and situations that feed fear and rejection instead of accepting and genuinely loving you merely for the inner person you are. You have to show the world who you are. You can only do this through serving your own soul first. Love yourself to the level you wish others to love you in return. Expand your self-love in selfless acts. It may be time to put the word "no" in your vocabulary gently adding that "it really doesn't work for me." This is honesty without being harsh. Get control of your mind, your emotions and your body.

Perhaps the most challenging aspect of life is to discover the divine within you. All you have to do is reach your hand up and pray for help to reach within in understanding yourself. Often this requires some kind of help from the outside which is professional in nature. We resist this. It is hard to clean the closet of your mind emotions and body.

It requires a consciousness shift and viewing your life with the help of a spiritual perspective with the teammates of reality and practicality. There are benefits to this work from the cognitive process. The light of your awareness shines forth like a brightly lit beacon and reflects the light of your divinity on the souls of others. Within your own healing, others are healed without you even knowing it. The healthy boundary of self-love is not selfish; it includes everyone. The gift is the discovery of your divine self. You court your own heart and fall in love with the new you.

Discovering authentic unconditional love is uncovering an aspect of you. Love must be welcomed and invited into your life. You reach into your own body so your spirit can light up all those little DNA particles of divine intelligence that holds the wholeness of love. This state of being which exists within you is ignited by the desire to remember this natural state of the soul. The soul sends a wake up call to every cell of your being to return to bliss, peace and happiness. This natural state has been referred to as living heaven on earth.

You yearn for happiness. Your heaven within your body your earthly being says here I am discover me again! As the higher heart of divine consciousness reaches to the heaven within, every cell of your being breathes a little more contentment in knowing it finally is all going to be okay. You regain faith in yourself. You remember the higher intelligence or the presence of divinity that lives within you. The soul calls forth peace and the state of being love returns. One day you wake up early in the morning and you feel something you cannot explain. Happy. For no reason at all you are happy smiling and full of life.

Your heart, the pillow for the soul, unfolds like a gorgeous light pink rose petal by petal to the pure joy of being alive. Imagine that!

Sharing Love with Others

esire comes from the soul. Wants come from the mind. Needs come from the physical.

We need air to breathe and water to survive from the physical realm. Our mind says I want this I want that. The place to start to get the best result in the long run is spiritual desires. However, humanity being as it is sometimes, often gets the order reversed and only focuses on the physical.

We exist in planes of awareness or states of being. They are referred to as spiritual, mental, emotional and physical planes of awareness. These are also referred to as the houses of heaven and the dimensions of the Universe. They are here in your life as a field of vibration or energy that you float in and out of. You exist in your spirit your mind and thoughts as well as your feelings and needs. Think of yourself as a big spiral of light or slinky toy that moves up and down and like an accordion stretches out or shrinks or compresses. This is your divine energy expressing itself.

You are not just the body. You have a soul. You have a spirit on assignment for this lifetime. You have a mind and an ego. You have feelings. You have a body. They all have a purpose which is to serve you. You have a purpose to remember the desires of your spirit and soul known as your divine plan. This has nothing to do with religion although I am certain there are religious teachings that support this. I would love to hope so anyway.

Metaphysics mean beyond the physical. It is often thought of as a place somewhere 'out there'. Often we think of heaven or the Universe as out there as well. We also think that finding love with someone else is our answer. Hopefully at this point you can embrace the possibility that out there is actually 'in here' meaning inside of you. How do you desire to share love with others?

Desire is the soul saying let us strive for this. After all you did agree when you signed up for life again in the divine plan that you would desire love. Your soul would long for you the person, whether you are man or woman, to remember what you are made of: Love.

Love desires to replicate itself. Love desires to expand to reach the interior sacred heart of yourself and in divine timing to reach out and share itself. You desire to be happy.

Your mind says yes but to be happy I have to have someone in my life that can make me happy. Really? You can't do this for yourself with all that love that lives inside of you?

So the first struggle of the mind shows up. We have a lower mind often called the ego and we have a higher mind referred to as the higher mind or superconsciousness. We need them both. The ego gets a bad rap sometimes. The ego keeps you grounded in that beautiful body of yours. It tells the soul, " Look, today we just need to be practical. You have to get up out of bed, stop feeling sorry for yourself, slap on a smile on that face and let's get moving. Life is waiting. Stop being so lazy in sharing love. It is after all what you said you wanted before you were born. To live, laugh and love." The higher mind the part of your soul that says, "Okay don't be such a pest. I will do this when I am inspired and know the timing is right. I will get out of bed. I will smile. I will go for a walk and I will breathe in the joy that awaits me with every single step." The two minds become partners in the practical and the spiritual. Very gently this partnership of heart and head starts to realize that happiness is a choice.

Misery is optional. It's up to you and your mind to decide. The soul ignites the desire the mind starts thinking about that desire and now your feelings kick in. How would that actually feel to be happy for no reason at all other than to be alive, really alive? Wow that would feel pretty darn amazing. I might just want to stay put and have a soul affair with myself. I give myself permission to be happy without anyone else. If that is where you are, then you have arrived at an amazing point in your own growth as a person and evolution as a soul. Then this other thought may or may not show up.

Maybe if I could actually feel love and be happy I could actually have more of that. It could be endless. I could be a bliss bunny. Then in the physical world I live in I would not be lonely. I would be fine with being alone. Maybe more people who are happy and would love being with me would show up. I could think about sharing love in a new way with family, friends, my peers and just perhaps healing the relationships I already have.

I am not suggesting you dump everyone in your life unless you really need to as there is a great benefit in healing what you have and making it better. We all have relationship dynamics with people in our life even if it's the barista at Starbucks. So lets take a look at all of those relationships and how the lost art of loving and conscious courtship applies for you in your life one at a time.

Sacred Friendships

A friendship that is sacred is another pearl of wisdom you carry in your heart at all times. They may be few and far between but you know who they are. They love you unconditionally and sometimes are your greatest comfort in times of sorrow. How many times have you heard the expression if you can count your friends on one hand you are blessed? We have sacred friendships and we have acquaintances. You know the difference. Anything that is sacred in your life is wrapped in the light of love. Even friends can let you down and we have to forgive them for not being perfect. You can spiritualize a friendship that will remain with you your entire life.

I was so heartbroken when my best friend of 50 years died. Nancy and I had met in high school. Even though I had moved to the other side of the United States we spoke on the phone at least once or twice a week. I had not been to Connecticut nor seen Nancy in 18 years even though we spoke often. I had a strange feeling one summer that I just had to go back to Connecticut and see her for the holidays. I didn't know at that time how ill she was, but my love for her was calling me to her side. She opened the door to her home I was so familiar with and I thought she looked like she was 90 years old. I was so upset by the state of her health. I knew listening to the intuitive hit I had gotten was very wise.

She didn't want to talk to me about her health at all. She told me at one point she had not seen a doctor in 40 years. I was really upset now and asked her why. She actually said, "Let's not ruin your visit by talking about my health, OK?" I honored her request to zip my mouth; although, I was furious with her for neglecting her health so badly. Her daughter who knew me well asked me, "Aunt Johanna do you know something I don't know about my mom? Is that why you came for Thanksgiving?" I knew clearly she was dying but said nothing.

Six months later, I was on my honeymoon in Maui. I always called her no matter where I was. She informed me that she had cancer throughout her entire body and that she was not afraid to die. My poor husband had to put up with me bursting out into tears during our entire trip. She died two months later, and I still miss her to this day.

I feel we believe that our friends will always be there for us and no matter what they will never betray or hurt us. This is often not the case. I was hurt that my best friend never confided in me about her fears about doctors. I actually was totally pissed off at her for acting like everything was perfect for years when it was a mess. I expected something of her that just was not her reality. It was mine.

Lets take a look at developing friendships and what our expectations might be. Once again this requires a new set of spiritual glasses. Most people focus on what does not or has not worked. They hold a negative clipboard in their minds and use this checklist to see what is wrong with a person based on their perception of what should be rather than what is. What they don't have rather than what they do have. Once again negative reinforcement slaps us in the face and we see everything that will not work in a relationship even at the friendship level. Often we use conditional love even with a new friend who shows up. After all this is just you being you isn't it? This is an icy dicey place to live in.

You attract what you are even in the form of new or old friends. Don't be delusional and think this person is the perfect friend with no flaws. Throw that conditional love expectation right out the window. Nancy was not perfect yet she was always there for me.

I often wondered if I was really there for her at the level she needed. My younger son is her godchild. He knew how upset I was when she died. He told me, "Mom, Aunt Nancy started dying a long time ago. Her body just did what she told it to do." How did he know she had given up so long ago? Was it possible that Nancy's failing health was a mirror to my own heart health problems? It did not even register that I needed more health exams at that time. Yet exactly one year later on the day she died I was in an operating room and felt her there with me. I know when it is my time to cross over she will be the first one to greet me. This is the power of sacred friendship.

Our friends are there to love and support. After my surgeries I found out who my friends were. I also found out who my so-called friends were but I had to be OK with that.

Loving a friend unconditionally means you will accept a friend with all their flaws. This can often be a challenge. Sort through your closet of friendships and be mindful of what needs to be saved and what needs to go. When you judge someone else, you are judging an aspect of yourself. You do have to be a friend to have friends but at what cost? How can we handle those friends who are suffering? Is it really our job to be their therapist or mother when they continually talk about their failures rather than their successes?

There are multitudes of people who are walking on this earth feeling disappointed.

Disappointment is very real. It can create an overbearing sense of resentment failure being injured sad rejected and abandoned. Has humanity forgotten to be kind? This is fear based heavy energy that you can feel and actually weighs down the Over-Soul. You can actually feel this if you are aware and open. It is not unconditional love. You do not need to run away from every friend who is suffering. Perhaps in understanding this person you can heal a part of yourself.

How often have you met a friend who continually complains of all the disappointments they have had in relationships and is so invested in naming each and every single damaging experience? Gets a little tiring doesn't it? Each time a person relives a memory of the past they are in their spiritual history of their past. This is why it is so painful because they are stuck in remembering how painful these disappointing experiences were. Regarding friends who give you advice, whether you want it or not, consider that any advice that is given no matter how heartfelt can often be some one's own projection of their own stuff.

In some cases, the advice is wonderful; like jewels of wisdom. Other times a friend's advice can be mental daggers filled with their negative thoughts and really have nothing to do with you. If someone keeps sending you judgmental daggers simply say, "I know you love me and I appreciate your opinion." If you are feeling really brave with this friend you may want to say, "I do not feel that this is right for me and once gain I thank you for your concern." Then move on from the subject so you don't get into a huge debate with words.

Be mindful and aware that advice is often subjective instead of objective. As people often see the light of love reflected in another they can often see the reflection of fear reflected as well. It is important to know if the advice being given belongs to you or belongs to the experience of the other person. If you are struggling with issues in your life, go to the sacred friends who cherish you and bestow wisdom that makes sense.

A true friend is an authentic pearl that is precious to your heart. A false friend is a struggle for many and often disappoints the mind and the heart. Know the difference and practice the Law of Discernment so you do not scatter your pearls of wisdom before swine or those whose soul is asleep. Everyone has their own divine journey and their own karmic contract with the Universe. In the age of self reliance we all need to figure out our next move on our own with a loving hand guiding and protecting our heart and soul.

Keep love and friendships that are pure close, private and personal just like your relationship with the world of Spirit. I have found lately that more people are sorting through personal friendships and holding onto the precious pearls of true friends and drifting away from negative people who pull them down. Not all friends are intended to be with you forever and the ones who are precious will always be there no matter how far apart you live geographically.

Your life is sacred as are all relationships. If someone comes to you with a story about someone else, or a question about someone else, tell them to please go to the source.

There is an obvious double meaning here. You are encouraging them to go directly to the person to verify facts and you are also telling them to go to the source where all love as divine wholeness lives. Not everyone will get this yet this will register in the soul. This can be with family, friends, people you work with and on a personal level, private intimate relationships. You must be a friend to yourself first before you can be an authentic friend to someone else. If there is one thing that can affect adversely an authentic friendship, it is gossip. Relative to sacred friendships more than anything else stay away from gossip. It is one of the poisons that taints the soul. It is a negative force that shreds the heart emotionally.

We are all messengers of light. It is your job to reflect love onto everyone who crosses your path. Through the actions of how you live your life you tell a new story. If a friend or acquaintance is driving you nuts pray for them. You know what it feels like to watch a sunset with a group of friends, right? Everyone gets quiet. There is no profound discussion on the chemical gases in the air that caused that sunset, there is only a sigh viewing something touching. No words are necessary. You connect.

How do we help a friend who is suffering in the present moment? Here is a very simple way to get either yourself or that person who is driving you nuts talking about someone who disappointed them two years ago. Bring it current by asking this one question. "

How does this apply to where you are today?" Keep repeating that same question to take them out of the past and look at today. If someone is living in their history of the past they are stuck. Do you want them to remain stuck or to be the seeker of joy? How does this apply to where you are today as a statement to a sacred friendship that is faltering?

This encourages not only you to reflect on what you learned about yourself and your behavior from the past that needs to change but encourages the other person as well.

Often if we want friends around us to change we have to embrace change first. The first step to living in the present moment is to ask a shift to occur in your spirit, that glorious light that exists within, to show you the way. That is pretty simple. Ask and ye shall receive. It may not happen overnight and if you persist in resisting moving forward you will remain stuck in the heaviness of illusion. That is not your spiritual inheritance.

Knock on the door of your heart wake up your soul and stop being so serious that life is a burden. It is a joy to be alive, ask anyone who has had a near death experience.

It may be time to let go of friends that are stuck in the mud and want to stay there. If you feel this is holding you back and change is not eminent consider gently letting go. Spend less time with them if you can—without being caustic or mean. If they ask you why, be honest and lovingly tell them how hard it is to be around the old story. Always tell them you love them. If the old story continues, you know what to do. Maybe they just needed you to tell them you love them, you care about them and you realize how stuck they are.

Again, this is the age of self reliance so it isn't your job to heal them. Heal what you have with them by being honest so you don't hold onto resentment. It is a step forward to a happier relationship with that person. I spoke about friends first because often we are closer to our friends than we are to our family. Yet a family member can also be a wonderful friend and if you have that, you are doubly blessed.

The Family Paradigm

Once again, it is not your role to heal your entire family. Sometimes just being in a family is work enough. There is a great opportunity to heal yourself and the dynamic of interaction within the family if you practice self-love as a shining example. Hopefully your example will help the changes that are needed within the family dynamic. Do not play referee unless you think and feel that is a role that is serving your soul. Personally, I feel it is a dangerous place to be in the middle of a conflict of any kind. Get off the battlefield if there is one in your family and pray for every soul. We all want to be loved for who we are as a unique child of the Universe. I would like to believe that the love and acceptance of our special self would be embraced by our family. You are very lucky if you have a family that wise.

We have a variety of families. We have our birth family our earth family or extended family of friends and peers and our spiritual family. We make a decision to be born into a certain family based on our divine plan. We actually chose this family believe it or not. 'You have got to be kidding', I sense you thinking but it is true. You chose a birth family group of souls to support your divine plan. Your parents are the role models of growth that show you female / male and they are your first teachers. Unfortunately, many families have gone through the process of dysfunction. I hope you have gained a pearl of wisdom and moved beyond duplicating that dysfunction in your own life. This is when you seek wisdom from outside of yourself that is professional and objective.

Many people are walking in the shadows of their soul's sadness in family groups that are painful. There is a choice to continue the pain or gain wisdom to move away from the pain. There is usually emotional drama and at some point it will act itself out. You cannot heal this kind of pain without help. Remember that.

I always felt like the weird one in my family. I am sure a lot of you can relate to this. My two sisters were very close and often I felt like odd one out but I did chose this after all.

There is a spiritual teaching that says there is one spiritual rebel that is born into a family to stir up the pot. It is the pot of stewed karma that is related to the family karma which has tons of ingredients in it. The spiritual rebel which I am pretty sure I was in my family also has a job to do. The job of the spiritual rebel in the family is to activate a new way of thought or consciousness shift. Specifically and simply their role is to move the entire family to a place of unconditional love to shift the group karma. It can feel like one heck of a job.

Many times you are born into a family with souls that you experienced before in another life before and have to work out some of the karma. Again, not all karma or unfinished business is bad; some is just a longing to continue a life with someone you really loved from another lifetime. As a child you just can't seem to understand why no one gets who you are. Then as a teenager you can get a little testy know what I mean? I never talked about my woo-woo experiences with my family until I was older and even then they were rejected. My son often said to me, "How on earth were you born into this family? You are nothing like your sisters."

I tried for many years to heal the karma in my family to no avail. If I were to record in my higher mind and soul the heartache that came from the pain I suffered from being rejected by this birth family, it would take a hundred years. Yet I did survive and have amazing sisters in my female friends. Thank God for that replacement value where I am loved for who I am and not judged.

My intentions with my birth sisters were totally and completely misunderstood. When my older sister was dying with cancer, I sent her books on healing and was told not to do that, so I stopped. I was not welcomed to visit her in the hospital. My desire for her to heal was not her desire to heal.

One day while I was living in Sedona, Arizona I was driving up from a little town called Cottonwood and heard, "She will die in February." I heard it then dismissed it because obviously I could do nothing about this. I was not surprised when my son called me in February to tell me my sister had died. I did call her home and asked to speak to my other sister and was told no one wanted to talk to me. Break my heart again, why don't you, Sister? This was another scar of pain that registered in my heart. I was able however to say this, "She was my sister too." Sadly, I was not invited to my sister's funeral because at this point in my life my birth family had no relationship with me. Can you possibly imagine what it felt like thinking I even needed to be invited to my own sister's funeral?

This was pretty pathological now that I really review that heartache. Yet I was not informed of anything other than via my older son when they called him to say she had died. That was it. No consolation no concern absolutely nothing besides being told no one wanted to talk to me when I called their family home.

I did my own crossing over ceremony with a special group of spiritual sisters who lived in Sedona at that time. I really did feel the love in the room and the presence of my sister's spirit. I knew my sister had finally arrived in her spiritual home. Relative to the other members of the living family this was a tremendous sadness on my soul. Finally I just accepted that I would not be understood or accepted which was what I wanted.

Oddly enough, in past life regressions, I discovered the family karma relationships with my parents and my sisters which helped me accept why I was thrown out of the tribe.

Apparently it had to be repeated so I could create my own spiritual tribe or family which 48

I have done beautifully. I went to therapy for many years to heal my own heart around this and realized how caustic this was for my own soul. I lifted the veil of disappointment and actually my deceased sister came to visit me many times to tell me how much she loved me. This was all I needed because I had a spiritual family that spoke to me all the time in meditation and visions. This first connection to spirit started at age ten.

My sleepwalking was a means to reach out to spirit. I came from a highly educated brilliant family with rigid viewpoints. I tried once to talk to my two MIT graduate brothers-in-law about quantum physics and the magnetic field which I had been studying in my spiritual development classes. They looked at me like I had two heads. I had to let it go. This was not the tribe that welcomed me. I know this may feel very sad to many of you but I really need you to know I am okay with this. I have a wonderful family with my husband and my two sons. I have thousands of spiritual children around the globe who often refer to me as their spiritual mother and this is more than enough. I am loved merely for who I am not what someone else wants me to be. At this point in my evolution, that would be rather impossible!

I am not an expert at counseling families so all I really want to say is regarding your birth family the main ingredient for sharing love is acceptance. Accept each other for who you are with all the imperfections. Let go of your need to be right or understood.

Love their uniqueness. The Universe understands and loves you. Your soul knows you.

That is really all you need to navigate this pathway of sharing love and healing what you have. You can't make anyone love or understand you. You can only love and understand yourself.

The People You Work With

I worked in corporate America and specifically health care financial administration for a large hospital system by day for many years. At night and on the weekends, I did my spiritual work. I used my vacation time to hold seminars. I was always working.

This playground of the soul in the world of business challenged every single spiritual belief I had. I created a family with the people who worked with me in my department by allowing them to be unique and express their thoughts without judging them. I was able to maximize their gifts and pointed out where those gifts were. My immediate boss told me once, "You have got to stop promoting people because you will then have to continually re-train someone new." Why would I not want someone to improve their life?

We had a saying in my department: pretend that whomever you are talking to on the other end of that phone about their medical bill is your grandmother whom you adore. Be kind, be loving, and be understanding. A situation can be difficult but that doesn't mean a person has to be.

How do you manage sharing your spiritual light with peers at work? How can you maintain spiritual integrity? This is not a race to step over some one's back. If the spirit of the unity of community is not there, review your options. You can heal what you have even in the workplace. Look at what you do love about your job. Affirm what you do love about the people who work with you just like that quirky birth family of yours. There is a definite need for a major consciousness shift in the corporate world.

We have to turn that world from one of survival of the fittest to one of thriving as an organized family. We have to apply the spiritual principles of cooperation consideration and kindness. Can the ego let go of the need to be right all the time? Beyond that, each day at least three times a day, unplug from the world of corporate chaos. Take one little minute to take a breath, focus on something that makes you smile get up from your desk and move into the flow of the divine. Find the time and make it a habit.

I worked for a man once who had a Bible on his desk front and center which was rather surprising in itself. He had all these financial charts like wallpaper all over his office.

They were also in the hallways so unless you were blind you looked at them each day.

He pointed out the failures not the successes. We obviously did not agree on how to manage people. He always told me, "The only thing that counts is the bottom line."

Really? I told him once I felt that if he were supportive of the people in his departments and looked at them like people instead of a number, he would get that bottom line result.

One day I had just had enough. You know what that feels like at work, right? I put my hand on the Bible when I walked into his office because I respected the teachings. I looked him in the eyes and said,

"What would Jesus do?" He started to cry. He told me how hard his job was and that he was under a lot of pressure. I understood that and I felt we really connected. I asked how I could help him. I came away feeling so free of this tug of war between us. I felt wonderful actually that things would improve. However, to my chagrin the next day, he was worse than ever. Fear won, Jesus lost. I left that job and refer to it as my corporate crash. In retrospect I think the Universe was kicking me in the butt to get out of there. It was so painful and uncomfortable that I had to leave and do my spiritual work exclusively. That one event pushed me into working full time for spirit. It was the best career move I had ever made.

I am not suggesting you quit your job. You have bills to pay. You need to realistic and practical. What I am suggesting is to seek the spiritual essence of cooperation in your workplace. Stop complaining and gossiping and see what you can personally change regarding being territorial. Find out what the corporate mission is in serving others. Are they philanthropic? Is there a desire in their products or service to do something for the greater good as an end result? Can you find the greater good in the corporate mentality where you work? Review this. If you are an instrument of change, then start with one little change. Change your attitude about your job. See where the spirit of unity and cooperation has the potential to create a family that works together in peace rather than war. If you are suffering, it is time to reach your hand up once again. Ask for help and be inspired by your soul.

The laughter of the Infinite God must vibrate through your smile. Let the breeze of His love spread your smiles in the hearts of men. Their fire will be contagious.

—Paramahansa Yogananda

PART III
CONSCIOUS COURTSHIP

What is Conscious Courtship?

Courtship appears to be a somewhat old-fashioned word. At least this is what the Internet Webster Dictionary said. The online dictionary furthers states that courtship represents the activities that occur when people are developing a romantic relationship that could lead to marriage or the period of time when such activities occur. I would assume that would mean the merging in the middle of two souls that have a divine marriage or connection—but what do I know? I think we need a re-do for online meanings of words because we definitely need a more current meaning for the word courtship.

No wonder we have lost the art of loving if courtship is considered anything old, outdated or antique. Courtship brings to mind an old way of behaving, yet it is not so. When you court your own heart, you are opening your soul to loving yourself in a profound new way. What if you want to share that loving with someone else?

Have we lost the need for courtship? If something has aged, do we throw it away? Like the elders of our prior and current generations, do we consider something old no longer valuable? Have we relegated the concept of relationship courtship to a time that no longer exists? The dictionary also states that "to court means to woo".

As I often joke, I work in the "woo-woo world"—this is actually perfect! In order to court another we have to woo ourselves first individually.

Conscious courtship is an intentional desire to court woo and discover love where it best serves your soul. The soul is the central source of all love. Your own unique soul is connected to the source of all that is; a continuation or a greater source of divine wholeness. Additionally, being conscious means being awake and aware of the laws of cause and effect. There is a vibrational activation of energy through this conscious thought feeling or act and how this activates the balancing of karma. Karma is unfinished business that you bring forth from another lifetime or create in this lifetime.

Karma is not good or bad, right or wrong it just is the memory of experience we have stored in the cells of our soul. The soul has memory of these experiences because your soul is the compilation of all lifetimes of experience. When there has been a karmic correction or a change of conscious courtship and we start to think, feel, or act differently, there is a karmic correction or adjustment. There is an expansion of your conscious self and evolution or growth of the soul which occurs even if one little tiny step at a time.

The benefit of this, also known as the beneficial reward from the Universe, through cause and effect (for every action there is a reaction) is that you have called in some tangible benefits. Does it mean a new Porsche will suddenly appear in your driveway? No. But it can mean you have more opportunities personally in your life to choose from. The rest is up to you and your freewill choices. We live in the present moment of today or at least we hope we do. We have spiritual work to do in making a correction or adjustment to improve our lives and all we need to do is to remember you are not stuck in any karma from the past. You can gain wisdom through doing it differently with better results which I often refer to as the karmic kick or result of your changes. You can consciously leave the past in the past and focus on a healthier way of living your life. You court your own soul first then the soul of another.

The center of your heart calls forth self-love sharing love with others and Universal love. Is the story of conscious courtship written on the pages of your divine plan? If you feel the pages are blank how about a new story yet to told? You signed up for life to experience love and to serve. You have to fill in the rest of the story with the main character in your play of life which is you. You are the hero or the heroine, the thief of love or the generous king or queen in the kingdom of sharing love. In other words, you have to begin with you and your ability to love yourself first. Do not for a moment confuse this with being selfish. Love that is soul centered is not self centered. Courting the soul is a conscious choice for inner happiness for yourself first. It is not being selfish. It is very possible when you start to shift and change the way you consciously live your life others will be affected. Someone who is invested in you staying stuck right along them at some point will either think or tell you that you are selfish. You can heal what you have and stay or you may feel it is time for courtship to have a new face and a new place.

The Dating Dilemma

To date or not date; that is the question. I had stopped dating after almost thirty years of being divorced. I had no desire, no want and no need. Dating is often referred to as discovery. What I discovered was that I could embrace dating or not dating as a conscious choice. I unplugged from all of this because after all I had all I desired wanted or needed. I had love all the time. I breathed it in. I tasted it and I felt great. I was very happy and content. The thing I wanted to was to to date myself and so I did. I had surrendered to aging gracefully without a life partner. It was such a sense of freedom with no regrets or feeling like I was missing anything or anyone. There is a big difference between being lonely and being alone. I enjoyed my work and my own company. I was not lonely and loved my alone time. I had the entire Universe after all with me each and every day.

Divine intervention then presented itself and said, "You are not done with dating." "Oh yes I am, are you kidding me? I do not want to do this. It doesn't matter, we want you to.

We desire you to. You have to follow your divine plan. After all, don't you remember, we remind you once again that your astrological chart said two marriages. A second marriage later in life. It is later in life and it is time. Well I do have a marriage. I have a divine marriage that is all I need. Let us remind you the voices from the other side stated that the lines on your right hand say long life and two marriages. Remember the break in the line around mid thirties?" Urgh. Yes, I remembered dating after my divorce.

My heartbreak of a divorce at age 36. I didn't forget that. It was a major heartbreak on my soul for too many years. Conversely, when I review this from a spiritual point of view it served an amazing purpose. I actually was grateful for that divorce you know because look at the path I took after that. I committed to working exclusively for the world of spiritual service. I also know I can re-write my divine plan and I can change it with freewill if I want to. "Yes but you always said very clearly, 'thy will be done'. This is our will. Divine intention. You had better consider this. Are you taking my joy away I asked? Perhaps there is even more joy waiting. After all, said the voice, everyone deserves a second chance at love. Think about that one." So now dear reader I do have to talk to you about dating and relationships. How to share the lost art of loving with a partner and allow courtship once again. At least this is what I am instructed to do. So I will.

I was engaged at 19 married at 21 and divorced at 36. This was a major heartache for me that I carried around like a rock in my heart for a long time. My heart actually ached and hurt. (I often wonder if my heart surgeries helped me release some of that heartache.

I hope so.) I had met my first husband when I was fifteen years old. We created two wonderful sons and if I am to look at any blessings from that marriage, they would be it. I also am not going to trash my ex-husband because he really is a good guy. We were very young did not have many coping skills in a marriage for the bumps in the road and rushed into getting a divorce. Getting a divorce will not solve your problems. It may actually add to them. I jumped into dating with many expectations. Everyone told me that I would get married again right away. I did not stop dating like a crazy woman. The dilemma for me was it was fun exhausting and often disappointing.

If someone goes into dating thinking it may not work out, it probably won't. People jump too soon from dating into marriage and divorce is their escape plan. I am not against divorce but I do feel it is too easy to walk away from a partnership without doing the work to make it better. It is so clear to me in second chances at relationships that we have to change our habits to get a better result. I have a number of female friends who have been married a long time. A large majority of them have told me that at some point in their marriage, they thought about divorce. They also talked to me about the world of dating. I told them it is not so glamorous. Now they are very glad they stayed and worked through the belief that the grass is greener on the other side. As a friend once told me, the grass is not greener it is the same color of brown.

Wherever you go, there you are along with all your stuff you didn't work out previously.

Don't take it into the world of dating if you do decide to make a change. Work on your stuff. If you are single, take a break from dating and go within to make those changes.

If you are in a committed dating partnership of some kind, take a spiritual inner retreat from the conflicts in your relationship if they exist and work on yourself. Try to detach and not talk about what is wrong with your partner all the time. Its very exhausting and heavy energy on your heart to do this over and over again. Obviously if you are in an emotionally, physically or mentally abusive relationship with a partner who is so rigid they continue their abuse, it's time to make a plan to consciously leave. Every relationship hits obstacles and challenges. It's part of life. It's an opportunity to grow and evolve not only on a personal level but on a partnership level as well. It can feel like a dilemma to stay single, consider dating, or leave a marriage. Dating is discovery. Date yourself first then see where you are.

This new temple of learning, a relationship, is probably the most profound sacred space to evolve within. It can also feel like the therapy couch of the Universe that you never got off of, but it is worth the effort. It takes dedication and devotion to live from a loving place to share that fully with another. We fall in love with the divine light that our soul reflects onto another.

This works really well for about 90 days because you see everything that you have in common; you see your own light reflected back. Then the honeymoon is over and the stuff made of fear shows up. Now you start to see everything that is wrong with this other person. What you are seeing acted out are your own fears. This is when we have to touch into the field of partnered love and bring more understanding into the relationship and your reaction to it. Many people feel they should not go to bed mad at each other which is probably a good thought. However, if you go to bed, have sex, then get up and are still mad at each other, what have you really accomplished other than your body feeling good? Not a whole lot. You have to communicate from your soul to connect with your body, mind, and spirit. You may not agree on everything, which is fine, and hopefully you can at least honor and respect the other person's opinion.

We all want love. We desire respect, attention, acknowledgment and appreciation. If you are in a relationship, are those present in your daily interactions? Rushing into leaving a relationship too soon is painful. If you are able to heal what you have, and have the desire to do so, review where you can change your habits of emotional knee-jerk reaction that causes damage. You will never agree on everything and at least you can start with a place of remembering why you came together in the first place: to share divine love. Love is not stagnant. It is a moveable feast of emotions and can carry you to a loving sweet refinement of loving in a whole new way. Conscious courtship in a dating relationship requires the awareness each day that you are a divine soul inviting the presence of more divine love, to give and receive with another soul. Give yourself time to learn about the other person. Love is love; it merely is. It has nothing to do with being a man or woman, it is just love. If you are in a relationship, try to see where you are right now or where you would like to be. If you are beginning a dating relationship consider this a new friend you are spending time with and nothing more.

The Cyber Bar of Online Dating

Yes, I had tried those dating sites and actually did meet some wonderful men. I was a little tired of repeating my personal credentials when I meet someone. I felt like I was handing in a resume at a job interview. I actually enjoyed meeting a new friend because that is how I approached it. I did not have a list of requirements and as a result met some interesting people. The world has evolved to such an age of technology that instead of going to the bars of old to meet someone dating sites have become the new cyber bar.

My friend Joanne and I thought it might a good idea to write a book about online dating a few years ago because we thought it would make for good reading. The same men were emailing the same exact messages to both of us. It was after all efficient to cut and paste from their point of view I would imagine. It was a numbers game. A game it truly felt like and sometimes we didn't feel like winners. Sort of like roulette; you place a chip down on a large variety of different numbers and hope one hits. Dating for each of us became a huge gamble. How can someone connect with another person who is seeking love consciously through dating sites?

After Joanne and I started sharing our stories with each other, we decided to dump the idea because we weren't sure how this would help anyone. We laughed so much we almost, well you know the saying. She shared such hysterical stories of dates I thought maybe we should write a comedy book. When we seriously discussed it, however, we also talked about what sharing love would really feel like after all those interesting dates. Joanne was on a spiritual path herself and actually I met her when I was teaching a spiritual seminar while living in Sedona. We looked at each other and both said how do we define love as a gift from the Universe? Where are we in resistance and if so where?

How do we use technology as a tool for sharing divine love with another? How does anyone maneuver the crowd of people in this cyber bar?

These were good questions and reminded us both that we needed to reflect on what was working in our lives without becoming disappointed. The laughter plugged us into our joy of being alive. We understood the cosmic joke and we needed to remember what the soul and mind already agreed on. I think men and women need to give each other a break and not take all of this so seriously. Oddly enough in the long run, the joke on me was that I met my second husband through Match.com. I could not figure out how his email came through when I had erased my profile completely. I was done with dating. I actually was thrilled to accept my relationship with divine love as the blessing it was. I had come to a place of accepting that my life was perfect. Joanne and I both agreed at one point that online dating could possibly be all about divine intervention. How is that for karma in making fun of online dating?

I know the Internet is a wonderful place to connect with someone new and you have to be realistic. Remember practical realistic and spiritual? Let's go back to the basics. It takes time to develop a friendship into something greater if you so desire. It takes energy to find quality time to include that person in your life. You invite them in and you welcome them to discover you. This does not mean you immediately invite a stranger to your home and cook them dinner with lots of wine on the first date. If you want to be courted, then allow the other person to court you. Negotiating a relationship is like planning a trip. You need a map unless you drive intuitively and that could be interesting. Consider when you are meeting someone new you are merely meeting a friend. In negotiating a relationship you are also interviewing a person as well. Don't get me wrong, this is not a job interview or cross examination. You are getting to know this person and discovering whether you feel you want to spend more time with them. I remember meeting some dates and they had a list of questions with them. I often wondered where they got this list and tried to open up when answering these questions. I have to tell you at some point I would say I know you want to use your time efficiently and I applaud your time management skills. Is it possible we just talk and get to know each other? Sometimes it worked and other times it didn't—which was too bad, so sad. I know the dating sites have these guidelines laid out for you and honestly some of them are very good so pay attention.

You cannot fall in love over the telephone. At some point you really do need to meet in person. I feel that telephone dating can create an illusion or fantasy environment. You are setting yourself up possibly for a huge disappointment so try to meet when the time feels right. In the beginning of a relationship, the first step should be friendship. Try not to look for what is wrong, look for what is right. Set the clarity of your intention as to why you want to date in the first place. Maybe you want someone who can go hiking every weekend and that is important to you. If they hate hiking, don't ignore it. A great interview question is what do you do in your free time? More than that, when the other person is talking pay attention and listen. Don't interrupt. Do not talk about past relationships that broke your heart. That is living in the past and where did that get you?

Conversely, if the other person does this, consider asking this question; where are you now with your desire to date? This is about the two of you, not the memory of every person who came into the room with you from your past that didn't work out. Stay in the present moment and enjoy meeting a new friend. We are all spiritual brothers and sisters living our lives to the beset of our abilities. Please try to remember that when you start to judge.

Here are some suggestions if you do want to pursue on line dating. First of all, you cannot fall in love online or on the telephone as we discussed previously. You may be very attracted to someone and what they have written about themselves is wonderful. Its a good start to opening the door to sharing friendship and possibly long lasting love. The key word here is possibility. If you spend hours and hours emailing, doing face time like Skype be mindful of creating an illusion of fantasy instead of the world of reality.

Write your profile from an honest place including your age. I know some people are not honest about this and a part of me understands that. If you start a relationship by lying, how do you recover from that lie? My husband listed his age as ten years younger. He told me on the phone a year younger. I knew something was off and I didn't need to be a psychic to figure that one out. He told me what high school he went to. I looked him up on the Internet and saw his real age. At first I was annoyed and then I decided to give him a chance on our one hour date for carrot juice! He was so nervous about 20 minutes into the date. He leaned over and said I really need to tell you something. I didn't want to laugh but I said," It's okay. I am ten years older than I told you." He yelled so loudly enough for everyone at Jumbo's to turn around. I told him I already knew his age and that it was more important to me about his vitality for life than the age on his driver's license.

He got a pass on that one. I understood where he was coming from.

Remember you are here to develop a relationship based on friendship first. You are not signing up to be a therapist for anyone; that is not your job. Building a healthy relationship starts with being spontaneous and it does make sense to date someone who lives close. If you want to have time to go to a movie, a walk visit a museum or anything mutual make sure they live nearby so it is practical. Are you culturally compatible? Do you love to travel and if so where?

When meeting for the first time, and I remind you of this no matter how wonderful this person may be, it has to be a public place. Alcohol changes things remember that.

Probably a better idea to meet for a cup of tea or coffee than at a bar. It's all really up to you. Know your standards and keep to them. Above all else please practice the 12 Date Rule which I cover later. It will save you heartache and allow someone wonderful to court you the way the Universe intends which is honorably.

This is a time of inter-dependant relationships as opposed to co-dependent relationships.

You may have experienced needy people who cling like Velcro to your heart and bubble gum to your shoes. The first reaction is to get rid of them. It is an opportunity for your own evolution. Just be honest. Telling someone, "This is really what works for me. How do you feel about that?" can open doorways to soul communication for real harmony. No one other than you is your answer. Likewise, you do not want to be 'the' answer for someone else. It will drag you down emotionally like an anchor tied around your ankles. Instead of running, talk. After talking, listen. Listen from your heart not your head.

Co-dependant relationships are attached to the Piscean Age, the age of the victim.

Rampant with soul torture, this 'poor me' age was also the age of addictions and relationship addiction was high on the list. I believe and I hope that where you are in your life you have the wisdom to recognize relationship addiction. In the beginning it is amazing that someone wants to call you and check in with you every hour right? When you are in a meeting and have five text messages that say 'where are you?' it feels good right? The attention is just amazing that someone could love you so much they can't live without you. Read those sentences again and see what this really feels like because it is unhealthy and should be a major red flag.

It is not your job to fill the cup of another person's heart; that is their job. You are not their therapist or their parent. If you want an equal partner, inter-dependant relationship is the path to jog along. We need air to breathe and water to sustain our life. The air and water serve our souls. It is a partnership of service. When we desire love from a spiritual friendship and partnership perspective, we are creating the opportunity to birth forth an inter-dependant relationship.

Consider this. Each person on the earth is filled with a spiritual light. That light is independent and unique unto itself. You meet someone. You are attracted to that light of their spirit. They have a light. You have a light. A third light is created independent also by itself. The light when the two of you merge in friendship that can lead to building a relationship. Yet the light of each other remains intact always. One big bubble of light surrounds both of you and inside of that the individual light of each soul. You never lose yourself or give yourself to the other person because you understand your own blessed self.

You never disappear inside of a relationship. You have a life without this person i.e., your job, your family, your friends. You don't dump them just because you now have a love interest. Ever had a disappearing friend show up after a failed relationship ended?

See what I mean? Don't abandon your friends because you have a relationship, include them and find time for others. The more you are consciously aware of your own light and the light of your intended, you continue to nurture the light of love that surrounds you. The relationship grows brighter and stronger yet there you are; the two of you standing in your own light and life. You are still connected even if they took a trip for a month. You are not freaking out if they don't call you every day. The presence is always there.

Give it the time and attention that is needed when necessary so it remains balanced and healthy. This is inter-dependency in relationship. You are there for each other you support each other you love and cherish each other. You absolutely never abandon yourself. Ever.

Spiritual Pathways to Progressive Partnership

There are five levels of entering and remaining in a sacred relationship: friendship, dating, relationship, partnership and divine complement i.e., marriage or life commitment. Sometimes you may get stuck on one level or maybe you are not supposed to go beyond that level. Often you may go back and forth to various levels. As long as you know where you are and what tools need to be used to expand that relationship it doesn't matter. Each one of the levels of progression is sacred.

Racing through a relationship does not allow you to discover how two hearts are aligned and compatible. The awareness of where you are in each level is important in the conscious courtship of divine love. That is a personal choice. The distance between saying *how do you do* in level one, friendship, and level five, saying *I do*, in the divine complement of marriage vows is vast and filled with many lessons of wisdom. Give this time and stop rushing into commitment before you even really know this person as a friend.

All relationships should be built on spiritual friendship not spiritual hypocrisy. If you are in a relationship are you still friends? Do you need to go back and rediscover that friendship again? Do you consider that person a beloved? Is this someone who you will love even when you don't like what they are doing? When you are devoted to conscious courtship of your own heart and soul, do you allow others to see who you are when the time is appropriate? Are you really devoted to the discovery of each other or just sorting through your 'here is what is wrong with you' list?

There is great value in having friends. You get to understand the opposite sex and how you relate to them. If you are single and love being single and want to keep it that way, love your friends and love your life. There has been so much pressure on getting married and sometimes it isn't for everyone. Even just friendships are part of a progressive relationship. Some grow into valued lifetime friendships and some are acquaintances. Each has value. Although dating is discovery, any time you spend time with friends there is still a discovery occurring. In the Law of Discernment, you discern or discover which friends you wish to spend more time with based on many factors. You have to decide for yourself who has greatest value for your growth and evolution. You can also accept that some friends are there for fun and entertainment.

Each level of entering a relationship is like stepping on a ladder you are climbing or stones you are stepping on. It is a progressive pathway to partnership. Get rid of your mental clipboards because all they are filled with is judgment which comes from fear.

As human beings, we are tested all the time. Many people call this their life lessons. We do live in an earthly classroom. We also have the opportunity now in the age we live in to graduate into the University of the Universe with advanced degrees. The tests serve a great purpose. The school of life pushes your soul to a realization of the divine that dwells within not only in you but everyone. This schooling is an education to move you forward to greater peace and happiness. It allows the potential for spiritual growth in every single person who crosses your path. Whether you stay at the 'friends only' stage is up to you. You have the ability in anything you are judging to view the opposite.

This viewpoint is your opportunity to bring out the hidden divinity within yourself and that other person by being truly authentic. Seeing the best in someone and seeing life from their point of view is an opportunity for the development of tremendous respect.

Additionally, patience compassion and understanding has its rewards because a true friendship is built on the divine quality that exists within each soul.

In the past if you and your clipboard mentally started writing down all the flaws of a person, sit still for a moment. Go within to stillness and ask to see the opposite of the flaw. Now be quiet and allow a divine response to touch your heart. A shift may possibly occur and you begin to view this person with your spiritual glasses on rather your judgments. However, you do have free will and this is a choice. You can remain stuck with the mental clipboard, continuing to judge and never get what you want. The media has done a great job in feeding us with these clipboard judgments telling you what is wrong with you and everyone else around you. Love that is divinely intended cannot exist in fear. Meet a new acquaintance with an open mind and heart. You are meeting a new friend, not your next husband or wife. Even if the dating profile you read said they want marriage, for right now, they are a friend. If you are rediscovering that friendship in your current relationship, be receptive and allow change to exist.

The first pathway is the development of sacred friendship. We have discussed sacred friendship previously. The same concept in dating applies to building a friendship first.

You cannot have a sustainable dating or love relationship with longevity if you are not friends first. This is the spiritual foundation you are building where the house of your heart rests upon. It has to be solid because when the chips are down even though you have obstacles you are still friends. The goal is establishing a friendship first not marriage so please get rid of that idea. Men and women need to remember that being a friend and having a friend are two different things.

I am saying this to men and women. If you start a friendship with lies you are in deep trouble. Then the issue of trust shows up. You do not dump your entire life on the table when first meeting someone. You reveal gently who you are and find time to discover the other person. The establishment of a friendship in dating is the first level in the process of sharing love with someone who you welcome or invite into your life. There is no need to be needy. Life isn't a race. It's a journey that should be enjoyed. You may decide this isn't someone you wish to date but would love to have as a friend so be honest and tell them that. Don't ever lead anyone on, it's not cool. If at any time you are certain you don't want to pursue even a friendship, deliver the message with love.

You merely say, "This is not a relationship I wish to pursue, and I wish you the best."

Don't expound on that and be kind. You are not doing anybody favors by spending time with someone who wants more than you are willing to give. However if you are ready to move into level two, dating, then you are opening the door to the process of sharing love with another. There is a desire to spend more time and get to know each other and build on that friendship.

Pathway two is dating. You have developed a friendship and now you decide to date maybe not even exclusively but you have decided to spend more time together. You open your heart a little bit more. You are open to courting the soul of each other just like you courted your own heart in self love. Dating is an opportunity to discover an aspect of companionship and compatibility. It allows you both time to spend quality time in sharing your values and hopes for the future. This is a great time for talking and listening as well. Look for what is right not what is wrong. Try not to judge harshly if something goes wrong. Be open minded and mature enough to open up the lines of communication if you feel this is something you wish to pursue. Dating that is real is a combination of doing things together. Not everyone has to love what you like to do so be okay if someone passes on an event that might not interest them. Dating is time together, one on one, so be mindful of introducing a new person into your circle of friends too soon. This is a development phase in building to pathway three which is relationship. The evolved soul is mindful and aware that there is a part of dating where the soul is guiding the way.

Let it unfold gently as a journey of discovery. Have fun with this and look forward to those dates.

Relationship building is a significant step. You move out of the questioning and getting to know phase of dating into something more committed. You are not rushing out to buy rings or a wedding dress. However you are both in agreement there is something of value to be explored with potential for more in the future. One of the big relationship builders is learning to trust your decision to be with each other and to trust that other person with your heart as well.

You have been dating for awhile and you have decided there is really no one else you wish to spend time with other than your friends. By the way because you are in a relationship do not forget those friends. If you are contemplating moving into phase four of partnership, you do not have to be glued at the hip! I would encourage you however to remember that building a relationship is a sacred journey. Keep it close to your heart and stop discussing every little detail with your friends unless you want a lot of opinions coming back at you which can be confusing. Get excited about sharing this adventure and remember that anyone giving you advice could be projecting their own stuff onto your heart. Each one of these phases are unique and you may actually decide you are content and happy dating and that is all. So be honest with yourself at which phase you wish to move on to if at all.

It has been said that the first ninety days of dating is the honeymoon phase which is probably true. We get so excited about this wonderful person who is just like us. Then the perfect person isn't so perfect anymore and we start to see what we don't like. Try not to leave too soon you could regret that. Be open honest and speak from your point of view. Anything that is unresolved issues or baggage from another relationship could find its way into anything new. Just make sure you are not comparing. Give the person you are dating an opportunity to shine once again. Do not allow yourself to repeat old unhealthy patterns and get clear if you are. If you like drama ask yourself why.

Two adults can sit down and talk. Children scream and yell, but you did not sign up for that right? You have to believe in yourself and your ability to manifest love that matches the intention of your soul. This is how we build partnering of two souls committed to the honor and joy of loving fully without fear. Generally at some point in a partnership you begin to talk about what your life would be like together in the future. Your shared values and lifestyle are working well and there is a desire for a life commitment. This traditionally is marriage or a ceremony of some kind.

The fifth phase of progressive partnership is the divine complement. The divine complement is exactly what it says it is. This person is a complement to who and what you are already are. They do not complete you because you are already whole. This partner does not fill any missing holes. They are not your answer for anything other than sharing a life and love honestly. They have your back. This is spiritual friendship taken to the highest level. This is total commitment to creating a life together and honoring that commitment. It is a new way of sharing your life with another person without giving up your sense of inner soul freedom. There can be fear around this commitment and if there is once again talk about it. Don't ever go into a partnership or divine complement partnership with an escape plan. If you have a Plan B as a backup, you have already given yourself permission to fail at some level. This is guided by fear and not genuine love. Commit to be committed to your heart being cherished honored and building a home for your soul for the future. Let this path unfold like a winding field of flowers. It is a covenant of spiritual love not just a legal contract. Blessed by the Universe inviting you to enjoy this walk through life of two hearts hand in hand.

How to Negotiate a Relationship

I am a product of the women's movement which had many positive aspects to it. It did not mean we hate men. We wanted to be equal. Equal jobs and equal pay was a biggie.

We wanted to be independent and some of it was extreme. There were rallies bra burning and women found their voice. Some women also found their anger and shot it like an arrow to any male who crossed their path aimed directly at their crotch. I often wondered how it messed up our ability to negotiate our relationships.

The pendulum swung in a radical arc taking us to extremes as all social revolutions do. It got way out of hand. Men got very confused conflicted and they got angry too. We were messing up the idea of relationships and courtship. No one appeared to know what the new rules were or how to even treat or act with women. Men and women got even more confused at least some of us did. "Don't you dare open that car door for me. I can do it myself, " I said once to my first husband. "Do I open the door or not open the door, you decide," he said. In the rage of that revolutionary change, a push pull was created and everyone took their sides like fighters in a boxing ring. Now I see a movement today that is correcting the extremes and the pendulum is finding balance.

The good news is that the co-dependent unhealthy relationships and addictions have come to the surface for both men and women. Believe me there are many men who are emotionally abused in relationships who have found their voice too which is great. My male clients have told me "I just need her to tell me what she wants plain and simple.

Why can't she just be direct?" We have to understand that in tipping the scales of reform, some of the baby boomers got lost along the way. We started an inner journey of self discovery to return home to the individualized self. Along the way we began to speak a new language of the soul.

The good news now is that we are in a different type of revolution. This is spiritual revolution. The soul is seeking its balance in sharing love with another. Online dating can feel like another job. It can be a lot of work. There are too many choices and it can get tiring. Some people give up some people carry on and some do meet the divine complement of their soul to partner with. In this new age of healthy choices pick one that serves your soul. If you do want a relationship, be clear on your intention in meeting anyone new. Be mindful, aware and trust your pure intuition. Try not to bring your old relationship baggage into your new relationship by complaining about a previous partner.

That is toxic waste and will destroy any new chance of living and loving differently.

Men and women for that matter are not your enemy. We are spiritual brothers and sisters trying to live life to the best of our abilities. I was divorced for almost 30 years so was used to doing a lot of things without checking in with anyone. I became totally self-sufficient and was happy living that way. It's a big bonus to have a female or male friend to help without asking. Its a huge comfort to have spiritual sisters who are there when you need them. Now I have a husband who does open car doors for me and I like it. I know I can do it myself. I buy myself flowers all the time like I always did. My husband is not really big on doing this however he does surprise me sometimes. All I say is, "

That makes me so happy, thank you." He does show me love in his own way. I have to accept that this is how he continues to court me and negotiates love in our relationship. I do smile and say thank you when I get a new electronic device for my office although I am not a techie person. It's just him being him after all. Courtship is a continual way of showing the other person you care and appreciate them. It is not one sided nor should it be. If you feel you are doing things and trying to negotiate something, are you doing this because you want something? Are you truly navigating within this relationship consciously or manipulating it? Are you living in conditional or unconditional love?

It is important to feel appreciated with any small acts of love. I am filled with a lot of warmth when someone says 'I love you' for no reason. My female friends and I are pretty good at doing that. It is meant and it is genuine. It's like getting a hug from heaven when someone says for no reason at all, I love you. It definitely is a heart hug for me. We all want to be loved. You can have a balanced equal relationship with a man or a woman still holding your own thoughts, your own life and your own beliefs that are independent of that person. You don't have to agree on everything.

The Data Bank of Experience

$\mathcal{T}$he body holds energy and registers emotion. It doesn't define if it likes it or doesn't like it. It merely holds the memory and stores it as information. It is a data bank of experience. The physical realm which is your body is an emotional sponge that is also an instrument of divine love. When you build your life and any type of relationship focusing only on the physical realm you have totally missed the opportunity to reclaim the divine art of loving. In simple terms, too much time attention and energy is placed on the physical. It cannot be exclusive unto itself. It is like an empty box.

It is important not to put so much emphasize in the physical realm. The key to living and loving well is right intention. This does not mean you cannot enjoy the beauty of the physical world. It does not mean you cannot spend quality time enhancing the beauty that radiates from within your inner Universe. It does not mean you can never wear makeup again. It does not mean you will never have sex again. The perfected physical world is a reflection of the desire of the soul. These are the higher thoughts of the mind and the balanced emotions from your heart. It is the garden you get to play in. It is the playground of the angels and spirit where we get to enjoy the gifts of being alive. If you really and truly want to be happier and live in the garden of love filling every pore of your being, leave your physical needs for last.

All relationships, including the primary one with yourself, must start by going to the spiritual plane of awareness or the desire of the soul. I guarantee you that if you are only living from the physical plane you will be disappointed time and time again. Do you really want to feel that life is a total waste of time? I learned from over thirty years of listening to the stories of disappointed people who felt that life has let them down with broken hearts and damaged souls. "Why did God do this to me?" they ask. God did not do anything; you did. Now you can do it better by looking at what needs to change.

We are on overload with sex being shoved into our faces 24/7. If you are fine with that and think that this is the way into someone's heart for a commitment, go ahead jump into bed with someone on your first date. Get all those physical needs taken care of.

Forget about your desires to be happy and full of love. Call me in one month and tell me how it is going. Do you feel loved? Do you feel happy? Is your soul singing for joy?

Or do you feel empty and sad and wish life could be different? Are you disappointed?

Only you can answer this question. I am not lecturing you. Promiscuity does not equal happiness or soul evolution. I am not thumping the Bible here. I am speaking from years of experience with thousands of clients both women and men heterosexual and homosexual as well. Ages young and old. I sat bewildered listening to some of these tales of woe around sexual expectations. There is a part of me that understands the nature of primal passion. There is also another part that totally rejects the beast of sexual desire without any respect for the body that holds a soul.

This dance of sex versus love plays a huge part in our lives. We are smacked in the face with it every time we open a magazine turn on the TV or the Internet. In this age of entertainment we live in sex is sold everywhere. I am reminding you that there is a huge difference between sex and sacred love making where two souls come together to share their divine selves. One will disappoint you and one will fill you up. It's a choice. Once again, I urge you to go to your own soul first before you even attempt to share love with anyone else. No one will fill you up with love. They can only reflect back to you what you show up with. So show up with a full tank of love even for yourself even if celibacy is a personal choice. How do you handle this if you are new to dating or even marriage presents this challenge? How do you spiritualize your sex life?

The Twelve Date Rule
and Sacred Sex

Many years ago one of my spiritual teachers, Beatrex, initiated me into the sacred arts.

Beatrex gave me a very practical teaching. After my divorce, I was a total relationship junkie who complained a lot. Everyone was so tired of hearing my stories I am surprised they didn't strangle me. I had a lot to learn about the sacred art of loving. This may sound like a simple teaching but if you desire to do life differently you might want to consider this. It is about the physical plane of awareness and it is a process to follow if you want to share love with others and receive love equally in return. It is called the Twelve Date Rule.

Do not put this book down! You are not allowed to jump ship from here. You got this far so hang in there with me. If you are tired of hearing others complain about their love life and sex life show them this. Then your work is done. At least for now. Then you can work on yourself if you desire to do so. You do after all have freewill.

The Twelve Date Rule is simply this; no physical intimacies until you have had at least twelve dates give or take a few. The first reason for this is that your soul and your self are precious. You are a sacred being. All relationships that have value are not built in the physical plane of awareness. They are created in the world of spirit then the mind then the heart and then the body. It needs to be spirit mind emotions then body. The body needs to be last if you want a relationship to last. The second reason is that when you connect too quickly sexually like first date sex for instance it can ignite every single survival fear that you have.

The body is such an incredible creation. We often forget it is a container that holds your soul. It is a temple of light and it is sacred. Everything has a function both in the physical and spiritual worlds. What connects these two worlds, the physical and the ethereal, are spirals of light referred to as chakras. Chakra is an ancient Sanskrit word meaning gateway or doorway. We have seven chakras in the actual physical body that connect us with our etheric body. The root chakra or base of the spine is considered a gateway.

Think of your spinal column like a thermometer. Imagine that bright red energy ball of light at the bottom of the thermometer before you take your temperature. When you have sex for the sake of sex, this life force energy also known as prana stays stuck in the base of the spine and has no movement. This is connected to your sexual desires only. Sex for sex equals survival fears panic regret and sadness. It ignites fear and because it is a lower energy it creates more fear. How many times have you or a friend jumped into a sexual relationship only to be disappointed and uncertain? It is heart breaking to feel this.

If you want a relationship that has value and longevity, that pranic energy needs to move up the spinal column first into the heart and then the mind. Like a flow of warm red liquid filled with divine passion the divine spark is ignited and moves into the higher realms of head and heart. Now you have a connection of spirit besides the physical taking you up the ladder of light. This is like the thermometer connecting the entire being: the mind, the heart, and then the body.

I refer often to the spinal column as the superhighway of light. It has also been referred to as kundalini energy and kundalini rising. This is the pranic energy filled with electricity and awareness that something is actually happening. There can also be a sense of profound joy in this feeling. It is neurological in nature. People who have experienced near death experiences have actually watched that kundalini life force energy move up the spinal column and out of the top of their heads. This is way beyond sex. It is connecting with the life force on a whole other level and is available when love making is sacred.

Think of a ladder illuminated step by step. A spiritualized relationship needs time to develop a true connection and create soul harmony together. Take this time to become friends. Relationships that have long lasting value are created and built on spiritual friendship. Become friends first. Friendship is the foundation of creation and then you pour the glue of love in to secure it. You must take your time. It took time for you to know yourself didn't it? It is a journey of discovery that never ends. We are always seeking more wisdom. It takes time to know the other person as well. Do not rush into sex. Intimacy is more than that. It is a connection of two souls sharing their divine art of loving.

There is no need for anyone to fill you up. That is your job. What a profound joy to discover each other. Waiting for sacred lovemaking is worth it. Forget your mental check list. This may not be a life partner you are meeting yet it can be a friendship that will last forever. You are taking the time to get to know each other. Even if you have a sense this is 'the one', you still need time to catch up and align two souls. Allow yourself the grace of time of sacred discovery. You can blind your spiritual vision and awareness if you are not honoring your soul. Wouldn't you rather see things clearly instead of creating suffering and massive soul confusion? You can wait and create something magical. Once again this is your choice.

A psychologist told me once that men communicate through sex. This is their language.

It is not however always the road to eternal happiness. You know the difference between sex and lovemaking. I sure hope you do. One far outweighs the other for long term benefits.

Here is something you may want to practice. Before you meet someone, even a friend, arrive a few minutes early. Even if you are just doing a phone call for the first time, give yourself this gift. Sit quietly. Breathe in and out about six times. Calm yourself.

Imagine in your mind the color pink which is the vibration of joy and happiness. Focus on this color. Wrap yourself in this color. Think of this pink energy like spiritual gift wrap. Now imagine that you are extending this color like a handshake to the other person.

Keep breathing. If your mind is trying to figure things out, go back to breathing—up and down, that is all. Go to the color pink. Extend the color. Reach for the spirit of the other person. Mass proceeds matter remember that. You can feel the energy of someone before you even meet them. Keep breathing. Allow yourself to feel the presence of your spirit then go to the other person: "Show me" is all you need to say. Melt into the color.

You have the ability to do this first. Quiet yourself, then get ready for your meeting.

Our eyes can be the trickster. They connect us to the physical plane of awareness first.

Try to be receptive to who this person really is. Enjoy the meeting. Divine timing means you take your time to get to know this person's soul and if you are in alignment. By doing this you are gifting yourself and the other person something that many people have forgotten. It is the practice of the courtship of the body and making sacred love.

When I first met my second husband, who is very handsome and virile, he was very upset one day and I think ready to end our relationship. I had called him to say 'hi'. We had only been dating about a month. I knew something was wrong as he was tripping over his tongue on the phone. I asked him to come over to my house and tell me in person what was going on. Something precious can be lost in the electronic age of messaging and thoughts can be misunderstood on a regular basis. It is best to speak to each other in person rather than having miscommunication end a really nice relationship.

Basically he wanted to know if I had any interest in sex. I sat there on my peaceful patio looking at all the flowers blooming and I almost burst out laughing. Yet I knew I had to handle this delicately. "Well actually at this point in my life I am more interested in making love than sex," I said to him. "I would like to build a relationship with you that is built on friendship first. In order for me to do this, as a woman, I need to feel emotionally safe and secure. My desire is to create a spiritual friendship first. Consider this like a beautiful garden we are looking at. I had to plant those seeds water them and take care of them so the flowers could grow naturally. This is the type of relationship I want. I want a relationship with you planted in the seeds of friendship that when nurtured carefully can grow into something profound."

"Huh," he said, "what does that mean?" I told him, " It means that I need to take my time to get to know you to build a spiritual friendship before I have sex because that is the foundation I want. This builds trust. As a woman," I explained, "I need to feel emotionally and spiritually safe and secure." I figured what the heck I had nothing to lose at all. I needed to speak my truth as clearly as possible. If he runs out of my backyard screaming, he doesn't get me. I didn't want to be with someone just for sex.

I wanted a partnership that was based on spiritual principles. I wanted to build a future with him not just a moment in time. Luckily he 'got it' and said, "No problem, take your time; I can wait. Just let me know when you are ready!" In any event his fears were put to rest. I didn't insult him, and it actually brought us closer together.

Do not rush into sex to seal the deal. You will fail yourself by selling yourself short.

The same thing goes for men. I have men tell me that women are too aggressive. They immediately want to jump into bed. Many women conversely say I just want to meet a man who is a gentleman, a gentle man, an honorable man.

Then why are women attracted to the bad boys? Men who are boys who play with the hearts and souls of multiple women are not grown men. They are exactly what the words imply. They are playboys. This is an old expression but it is currently rampant. If you think for one minute you will tame this wild boy that loves to play, you are mistaken.

Unless a bolt of lightening brings him to his knees with a huge change of habits and lifestyle do not walk away; run. I know it's so tempting and if all you want once again is a few moments of lusty sex and the high of his testosterone go for it. If you want authentic love and a significant relationship where you are treasured for more than your body, you may want to rethink your choices of a boy versus a man. I am not talking age, I am talking maturity. As shocking as it may seem some women are doing the same play girl dance that the bad boys do. All I have to say to that is, "Sister, sister slow down and heal your heart."

I have a number of men in my practice who have the same complaints women have in the quality of choices out there in dating land. It may surprise you to read this but many men want a woman they are proud of. "I just want to meet a nice lady," they say. "A lady."

Men do not want women who trash talk. They do not respect women who talk like this and they do not want to introduce you to their family and friends. They want a woman who dresses without showing off every asset they have. They may want a one night stand with you but they won't court you. They want a woman they are proud to be with.

We have confused our roles sometimes. Women are too aggressive and men are too passive. Women want a man not a boy but they want to be in charge of where and how fast the relationship is going. Men want a soft sweet woman and they want a tigress in the bedroom. We push we pull we give up and we try again. Unless you define who you are, you cannot manifest what your soul desires. The law of cause and effect has to start with you. Hopefully men and women can create a peaceful garden to grow love with grace and ease. This is a change of habit that may be the best gift you have ever given your heart and soul. Respect your body.

If you meet someone new, and they immediately start talking about your body or the conversation is sexual in nature, tell them this is not appropriate. If this continues, tell them again, "I am seeking a relationship built on friendship and am more interested in making love than having sex. Do you know the difference?" We are physical beings and we are attracted to the chemistry of another person which is wonderful. It makes life juicy. We all want to be with someone we are physically attracted to. This is one of the nice things about having a physical body. The pleasure must be sacred and conscious.

It may sound old fashioned and let me remind you that your body really is a temple of sacred light. Take your time in courtship. Discover the heart of the other person.

Consider your heart to be like a rose. It has layers of petals. One petal at a time the rose gently opens its petals to the sun to receive warmth and sustenance. Think of your sacred heart as the pillow for your soul in the same way. One petal at a time you reveal your emotional self and invite the warmth of another into your heart.

I do feel the woman is the leader in the dance of love. Men are very good when you clearly speak from your heart directly and tell them specifically what works for you.

If my husband while we were dating had stormed out of my backyard when we were discussing sex versus sacred lovemaking, he wouldn't have been the one for me. You cannot be afraid of what someone thinks about you in how you communicate your true feelings. Intimacy is much more than sex or making love. It is sharing your inner most authentic self. It takes time. It takes maturity and soul evolution and hopefully that is the journey the seeker of the lost art of loving uncovers. I do believe that all women are goddesses waiting to be discovered and a man who is wise and a god in his own kingdom understands this. We are all gods and goddesses. I have found my male clients who are opened hearted and yearn for love seeking one thing; an honorable woman. I hear that all the time.

I know sometimes life feels like you are in a washing machine constantly in the spin cycle. I also know there are so many good soul inspired people who do want shared love.

Everyone desires to be respected and acknowledged. We all want to be appreciated. The words thank you and I understand go a long way for both men and women. It's all in the delivery.

The Money Game

We live in a material world. Matter is created in the form of reality that we can see touch, taste, hear and feel. The material world you live in, the physical realm of the earth, is a playground where all the senses are activated by your response to matter. It appears that what matters most to many is money. Those material possessions, although they may be viewed as a great accomplishment to measure your life by, have nothing to do with your soul. The physical realm is also considered to be the land of manifestation and results. It is the land of stuff. Money in and of itself is not bad. It is an energy system that moves goods and services and compensates our world of wants and needs. Money is an energy system of exchange. We give it a lot of power even in personal relationships. We also confuse money with fulfillment along the way. Often sex and money became the thieves of our divine soul.

The greatest value you have in your life is the energy system of discovering love through your inner bank account which is your emotional heart and soul. I don't care how much money is in your physical bank account. If you are not fulfilled within, you will be poor in the world. I have many very successful and wealthy clients of great status in the world.

I can tell you their money did not buy them any happiness. It merely gave them choices.

The world has gone through many changes in our financial systems significantly. In the United States the banking and mortgage industry failing was a good lesson for all of us to review our personal lifestyle value goals. We have invested so much time and energy in the gathering of things that we have forgotten the most precious part of life.

I do believe there is divine intention in many things and hopefully people are now reviewing what the value of money is in their life and what is important. The former workaholic is now finding more time for what he values most in spending time with his family. Money is merely a currency of energy. It does give you choices. It is also an opportunity to be of service to others. It does not make you happy forever. It is another type of instant gratification that is not long lasting. I also feel strongly that it can ruin relationships if not handled correctly and consciously. Money that is not consciously considered in a relationship can be used as a form of manipulation. The first place you may want to consider taking a look at is your own personal relationship with money and the value it has for you. The second focus should be putting that aside and really being honest with yourself. Does money fulfill you as a person? Even if you have little or no money, happiness that radiates from within costs nothing.

I know you probably have a standard of living that is important to you. There is a lot of value in living simply and we hear this all the time. What does that really mean for you personally? Right now many people have decided that enough is enough in being so materialistic that the real value of their life has disappeared. In this quest for living simply I merely wish to state one thing. You do not have to be poor to live simply. Living simply is living without complications not necessarily living in a tent with a begging bowl at your side. Living simply is living from a point of clearly knowing where your joy and happiness comes from other than your checking account or credit cards. Living simply means living wisely in all choices.

In order to live simply and have a life that is fairly uncomplicated take a moment and really be honest in answering this question. Have you at any time used money as a means of negotiating a relationship? This is not just for men it is for women too. It can mean family, friends, people you work with or a partner. Part of being in a relationship if you are sharing space together can also include sharing resources one of which is your financial relationship. This is probably one of the biggest challenges in any relationship.

How you each handle money and the value it has to you personally and as a couple cannot be neglected. How do you negotiate the money game into your daily life? It is also one of the biggest sources of conflict. Are you using money to manipulate? Are you using money to manipulate yourself into instant gratification? There is nothing wrong in enjoying beautiful things but do you really get soul satisfaction from them? Do you own them or do they own you? Are you living beyond your means trying to fill up your heart with the stuff? When is the stuff enough?

Once again my teacher and friend, Beatrex, told me this wonderful story many years ago that I have never forgotten. Money was originally created in the form of a round disc that was called a token. For any of you who have ridden a bus or a train you know what these tokens look like. This first form of money was not created to buy anything.

A person, generally a man in those ancient times of Babylonia, presented a woman with one of these discs as a token of their affection. This is a phrase many of you may already know. It was given to show the person you cared about them and nothing more.

Then human nature being what it can be put conditions on giving this token of affection.

Unconditional love became conditional. I will give you this token but I want something in return. I want your love your attention your commitment your body. You belong to me. We started trading unconditional love and love for the sake of pure love for a barter system.

If you are struggling in this world of crumbling economics, you have an opportunity to live a very wealthy life. If you seek happiness daily in positive thoughts and less through material possessions your heart and soul will be set free in the kingdom of total abundance. Remember the three fold journey of reality practicality and spirituality. Take a look around your home. Does everything there truly represent who you are today? Is there excess you can clear out? Remember once again that everything is energy. If the energy of your home, office or business does not truly reflect the inner quality of your clean and clear heart and soul maybe its time to clear out the old and bring in the new.

You don't have to spend millions to make this happen. Keep what you have if it is a reflection of what you want the world to see. Take the old stuff and pay it forward. You don't need to live an austere life with limitations. The value in clearing your material space is to give perspective to a new vision of how you project yourself out to the world. If you are using material possessions and money as a means to measure another person please put your spiritual glasses on and see the value and goodness of their soul. This is the greatest treasure chest of all.

The One / Soul Mates

There is no such thing as 'the one'. I hear this question all the time, "Is he or she the one?" The Universe never wrote anywhere about the one or soul mates in your divine plan. Man created that. I would encourage you not to get trapped into the one or soul mate thinking and here is why.

If you accept the concept that there was something missing when you were born, a quest for someone or something to fill up the missing part will be a journey that never ends. You will walk through life trying to find that perfect match instead of welcoming someone who is a compliment to the unique soul you already are. There is nothing missing from you when you are born; you are whole unto yourself. Do you actually believe that God made you with something missing?

I was raised Catholic and understand the concept of original sin. Basically what was drilled into me was that I was made imperfect in God's wheelhouse of creation. I struggled believing this even as a small child. So often I would sit in church on Sundays (mandatory attendance if you go to parochial grammar school) and would think God doesn't feel that way. Nope, I'm not buying that one. I kept my mouth shut however. I still felt that I had all the tools I needed to be successful. Maybe it was the innocence of childhood, but I felt I could do just about anything I wanted with the help of what was out there dancing in the arms of the Universe.

The search for a soul mate is saying to the Universe, " I will not be whole or perfect until I find this person who makes me complete. He completes me." Have you heard that before? The guides who work with me have told me many times throughout life a person has up to five to seven possible partners or opportunities to connect with what I refer to as the Divine Complement. This person is not a lost piece of you waiting to be stapled onto your heart. There is a balance and healthy aspect of a Divine Complement.

Regarding the number, you have a variety of opportunities in your life to learn a lot about yourself in this new temple of learning called relationships through the experiences you shared with this other person. No one on this earth is perfect. If they were perfect they would not have signed up for life to refine the experience to grow as a person, correct all karma through lessons learned and have soul evolution.

God did not say, "Okay you only get one shot at this so don't mess it up." You have more than one divine complement. Get out of fantasy and into reality and open your heart and mind. Compatibility and communication allows two adults to take their time to learn about each other and yourself and the process. Don't leave too soon if there is value there. If you have found yourself like a bouncing ball going back and forth to a relationship, stay and do the work. There is a blessing in everything and that blessing is wisdom. What you learn about yourself as your own 'one' allows you to continue to grow in your own light and share love that is honorable, respectful and worth the journey.

Try to avoid, in your quest in sharing love with another or healing what you currently have, pecking away at all the wrong things with every single choice that crosses your path until you meet that one, perfect match. Rushing away to find another 'one or soulmate' never solves anything. There is an alchemical shift that happens when you focus on the positive qualities and start to see the person in a new light. Then on some mystical magical level they do become the one that matches your sacred heart. You get to fall in love again and again not only with that person, but your choice of loving yourself in loving them.

How to Trust

"How can I ever trust again?" is a common question I hear across the telephone line in spiritual counseling sessions. Betrayal is often a wound that sits festering in the heart like a thorn you cannot seem to remove. It often feels like it will take lifetimes to heal.

What I know is this; trust is truly an act of faith. Not a faith in a religion or system of belief but simply the belief in myself. Even a person who feels they are spiritual has challenges. What I have observed through my own life process and those who are on a path of trusting in their inner wisdom is the emotional reaction to life challenges is different. Don't get me wrong, you have to take ownership and responsibility for your own choices and behavior. Although some people do, you cannot use your higher self as a cop out. The divine plan doesn't work that way. This is referred to as a consciousness shift or a new perspective in how we look at life in general and our role in that life. You put the spiritual glasses on and I don't mean rose colored glasses. I mean glasses that are clear and real. It does not mean you excuse the way you dance the dance of life in the real world.

Reality, practicality and spirituality are the new melodies for the pure song of the soul.

Without this three fold viewpoint working together, you are toast. Burnt out, fried, baked and done. Ready to give up. If you don't trust yourself in making wise choices it is almost impossible to trust someone else. The first step is you have to be realistic in the choices you make in your life. Its time to depart from fantasy land and live in the real world. Fantasies keep you in illusion and prevent the real you from showing up.

Haven't you wasted enough time dreaming what could be instead of trusting that what is may be just fine? Get real so you can heal. Trust has to start with you first. If you do not trust your own judgment, you will constantly double check not only yourself but the relationship with the other person as well. If you constantly look for something to go wrong, chances are eventually it will. What if you were to look for what is right instead?

You will only be able to trust another when you learn to know and trust yourself first.

Practicality seems like a pretty boring explanation for understanding trust and yet I do feel they do go hand in hand. Once you get real with your life as it is in the present moment you have a great opportunity to trust that your choices are practical. They have to make sense. You do not need to lose sight of a dream as long as you don't stay stuck in the illusion. Practical choices are the result of you being realistic with who you are and who you welcome into your life to share love with. This can be anyone in your relationship dynamic including friends family people at work and someone you have a personal intimate relationship with.

The issue of trust is huge in all relationship dynamics. Many people and perhaps you as well have experienced a trust that has been broken. In all areas of relationships where trust has been broken it causes the soul to suffer. Suffering creates more doubt and fear and now you really are in double trouble doubting everything. This is not exclusive to intimate relationships yet it appears this is the temple of learning where we struggle the most. In order to rebuild trust in someone else there needs to be a space of time to heal what has been broken. Generally what feels broken is your emotional heart and the ability to love and trust fully again. If you have decided to end a relationship as a result of a continual pattern of untruths and broken trust, take some time to regroup emotionally.

Rebuilding trust requires a number of elements. You cannot manifest or create something new until you get clear on the direction you want to travel with that other person. If you feel your back is up against the wall, take some out from any relationship interaction that continues to pick at an old wound. You have to find a way to emotionally detach without destroying a relationship forever. Think before you speak. Journal what your intentions are and if you can get some objective advice from a professional. I know as women in particular we love to get counseling from our female friends yet be mindful.

We often get advice that is not objective and is a projection of the other person's own relationship karma. You have enough of your own. This is a sacred time to heal what is real and practical. Then add some spiritual aspect to the healing process.

You are divinely intended to live from a loving place in your heart and soul and to have that returned in like kind from those who are precious to you. You can rebuild trust when you feel strong enough in your resolve to trust what you want to create in moving forward. Every time you refer to a broken trust or anger issue from the past, you break your heart a little more by allowing fear to be your guide. Trust that the purity of faith in your ability to give and receive love fully exists for you as a divine right. You have to determine realistically what that would like for you.

If you use the world of spirit as an excuse, you are not on the path of awareness. You certainly are not on the path of conscious courtship which advances you as a human being to the higher nature of your soul. This is known as the divine marriage of head and heart. Here is what I mean about using the world of spirit as an excuse. Some people use their religion or belief as a scapegoat. They blame it on God. I don't care what you call this but there is no such thing as being spiritually elite. If you were the one who broke a trust you have to take ownership and be honest. Someone told me once that they found their soul mate and were so happy that they finally met. They said they were divinely guided to each other and nothing would stand in their way of being together. Then they told me this person was married. After meeting this person once they decided to live together so they could continue on their souls journey together. "What could we possibly do? I was told spirit brought us together." This did not feel realistic or practical yet the excuse was spirit guided them to be together. A number of years later, when they separated, all karmic hell broke lose. There was tremendous damage control that needed to be put into play to repair another broken trust.

We do not have the right to judge another person's journey yet often I sit and scratch my head and heart asking why? Why do people continue to repeat old patterns expecting something different to show up? You do not need to struggle to find trust in your own heart. The first step is to allow a change of how you see your world realistically show up.

Please try to forget the TV commercials. They are illusions intended to entice you into believing that something or someone is missing from your life. Trust what your heart feels and let your mind follow.

Trust your choices in new relationships and give it time. Rebuilding trust in a damaged relationship is not an easy task. It is important to hold onto the belief that anything can be healed.

Heal What You Have

It is so easy to walk away from a relationship isn't it? Did you ever wish though that you had stayed? Did you ever think "maybe we could have learned from our mistakes or made it better?" Hindsight is just that; it keeps you in the past and disallows you to move forward. Regret is a weight of sadness you carry in your heart and soul. Based on many of the thousand of relationship stories I have heard from my private clients I feel there are many who regret leaving too soon. I know after speaking for awhile and pushing aside the tears they wish they had stayed and done their spiritual work. It is pretty obvious when you have to get out of an abusive relationship that is crushing your heart and soul.

Yet if there is a shred of doubt I encourage you to to pause and pay attention to your soul before you run out of the door of a relationship. The first step is to go back to the place of why you fell in love in the first place. Try to remember what that felt like. It is a good place to start.

It is such a heartache to hear all the stories when someone has cheated with another person, is addicted to pornography, or is emotionally abusive. You cannot heal this yourself. You have got to go to a professional to walk you through the stages of recovering from betrayal. If your partner refuses to go to therapy, then go yourself.

There are plenty of support groups for both men and women where you hopefully find the right environment to deal with your grief and the death of what was.

Not all relationships can have recovery but you can recover your own soul for yourself.

If there have been broken promises the need for forgiveness is needed. Forgive yourself first and work on you. If you have betrayed another you have to apologize and say you are sorry. Own your mistake. As minor as this sounds, it starts to move the energy of the soul towards healing and second chances. Be honest with yourself and honest with the Universe. Sometimes we see things not as they are but as we are. Love always brings understanding.

I would like to remind you of some spiritual principles that may help to rebuild the house that holds your own sacred heart.

- A spirit that is divinely guided knows that suffering does not belong to the soul.

- When you quiet the mind, your emotions will follow.

- The mind is the devil's playground or a temple of peace.

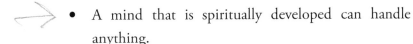- A mind that is spiritually developed can handle anything.

That is a choice, a perspective and a state of awareness. In order for your trust to be rebuilt please remember that it begins with the attitude of both people.

The healing of what you have starts with the inner journey as we have stated previously.

There are pathways to healing in this journey that almost make you start from scratch.

It has to start with how you approach your life with your attitude. You have heard about the attitude of gratitude right? Do you really live it though, I mean actively live it? For almost thirty years every single night before I close my eyes and every single morning as soon as I wake up before I get out of bed I say the same exact thing, "Thank you for all I have all I am receiving and all I am about to receive". What I really am saying is thank you for all past experiences including any past life karma that I needed to work out.

Thank you for everything I am experiencing in the present moment of the next 24 hours.

Thank you for the experiences of the future.

I am not saying "just give me the good stuff." We signed up for this life. We asked to grow as a person through life's ups and downs. No one ever promised it would be perfect. We have to be grateful for all experiences. The good along with bad teaches us everything and from that wisdom healing begins. It is your attitude and desire to evolve as a soul that activates continual healing. I encourage anyone to use that growth to open the doors to more awareness. Therein lay the good stuff! You will be both smart and wise in your attitude. They are excellent partners on the tennis court of life.

Review your attitude right now about your past. Anything there you need to heal? Try not to look at what was wrong with your past. Look at what you learned about yourself.

Look at where you are today. Are you repeating that story from the past? Is your life the same as it was ten years ago? Are you blaming others for the way your life is now?

Really? Don't judge yourself or others merely review your choices. If you are making choices that are clearly improving your life then you applied wisdom and your soul said yippee!

Put the book down, get out a piece of paper and write these words: Here is what I would like to change so I can heal my relationship. Then look at your attitude regarding what needs to change. Just pick one or two things. Don't overload your plate. You can do it.

Put your spiritual glasses on and look at reality practicality and the spiritual nature of your life. How can you soften your life? Life is a divine banquet. Eat and consume the experience only that serves your soul and makes sense for you. Review what is working for you, watch for the signs for the ticket to ultimate happiness which is to be free in your soul. Strengthen your soul, trust and believe in yourself embrace change and be free.

When both parties recalibrate thought and attitude, the energy shifts and you learn to heal, trust and love again. You may fall in love all over in a new way and have an even better relationship than you did before.

Set yourself free to thrive, not survive. Let go of the old story. You will be happy you did. Release regrets and disappointments, which is the anchor holding you down. It's a ton of baggage, a crate of craziness and it is not necessary to dance the new dance of life in your present moment. Now you are on your way to really healing what you have.

I am a recovering perfectionist. At least I am trying to be. If the dishes in the sink don't get washed right after breakfast, I really try not to freak out. In order to move to a greater sense of freedom I had to move from that idealistic perception of things being perfect to being realistic. It was not easy. I have to say it was a major struggle for me.

It was holding me back. When I worked in corporate health care, if I delegated a task to someone, I would sometimes take it back and re-do it the way I thought it should be-perfect. It created more work for me; my staff felt deflated at times and it slowed down everything. I had to let go of that one big time. I still like things neat and tidy and in their place. My husband loves to do laundry bless his soul. However, he forgets to fold the laundry, move the washing to the dryer that kind of thing. Sometimes I feel like I live in a laundromat. A very messy laundromat. Now I just close the door. When I need to do some laundry, I ask him to move things. Oddly, he does. He is a good follower of requests.

My perfectionism was getting in the way of feeling free to do anything else. It caused a lot of resentment and needed to be healed. After all I wanted to have a perfect house even though no one cared less about my laundry room! It took time, energy and was a good lesson in letting go of old habits and my attitude around them. One of my fears was if things in my house weren't perfect I was afraid people would judge me for not being perfect. I probably learned it from my mother but that is an old story. Her biggest fear was what will the neighbors think? When I said one day who cares, she was not pleased.

Fear is low energy, it keeps you stuck. Beyond that, when you empower fear you lose faith in yourself. I decided to love my imperfect life and oddly enough, without saying anything, the laundromat is now very organized.

The future will unfold beautifully for you if you take care of the present moment. Will there be challenges? Probably. So often clients ask me to take a peek into their future and many times it is around relationships. "Can this be healed" they ask? "What do I need to do to change my life?" In terms of 'seeing' what is before them as opportunities there appears to be a distinct variation in every vision. The future and the events that are foreseen are also referred to as probabilities and possibilities that are energetically directed by your actions. Surprise! Your freewill directs much of what occurs in your future. There is often the feeling in the divine plan that life is cut in stone and there are no choices. "This is my destiny" I hear. "I have to accept my destiny." This is rather a pessimistic escape hatch if you ask me.

You direct your destiny as the co-architect of your life. The Universe opened the playbook on your game of life and you created the moves often changing them in mid stream. This is why the actions you take, the thoughts you have, the feelings you operate under all have a direct influence as to the direction or path you future will or will not take. There is always that kind of mystery that comes with not knowing. I also hope it is a thrill of some kind knowing that you can change the playbook. You are only stuck if you believe you are stuck. You can heal anything if you really want to.

You want a future filled with love and loving people? Then you have to start doing things differently now. Present moment now, 24 hours now, not next week or next month.

When you are operating in your future wishing things could be different you lose the commitment to living in today. Don't dream away your life by wishing your future could be different. Allow it to be different by changing today. If things from the past keep coming up are you stuck in your old history? It is not healthy on any level if you keep picking away at something from the past. It can't heal. You are boring the heck out of everyone including your own soul.

Do you really want to live out your life stuck in the train station of life or would you like to be move forward to greater happiness? Do you dream and wish in future fantasy land hitting the ground with a thud when you realize that you aren't there yet? One foot in the past and another in future keeps you off balance in the precious moment of today. It robs your Over-Soul of increasing the magnetics to call in and draw love in a magnificent way. Do you really want to miss the train to your future by living in the past?

You have to heal a part of yourself and forgive yourself for not being perfect. The same forgiveness has to be given to your partner. Sorry but its true we are pretty imperfect human beings. Can you consciously forgive another for their mistakes or betrayals so can you move forward into the present moment? Can you fully let go and leave the past in the past to heal what you have? Do you have the foundation of love under your feet to build a new home of love? These are simple questions. What are your answers?

Second Chances at Love

You may have decided to heal what you have and if so I am thrilled for you. You have a second chance at loving yourself and your partner in a brand new way. Then again maybe you are beyond the point of no return and are now single. Whether you decide to date, spend time with your friends or are happy alone, you have to realize that this is a personal spiritual choice. The world has enough pressures and sharing love should feel like another part of your journey to be enjoyed. You have an opportunity to discover the path of recapturing the lost art of loving in whatever form works best for you.

After experiencing a divorce that brought me to my knees screaming to the Universe to help me, I started on a journey that led me to being truly happy without anyone by my side. It did not however happen overnight. I had enough dating to last me ten lifetimes.

I was a dating junkie for a long time and probably a relationship addict as well. Yet I threw myself into the dating swimming pool time and time again with the hope and belief that I was not intended to be without a partner. After all on the Noah's arc, it was two by two right? Wasn't that the natural order of things in pairs? However, putting that theory aside, I embraced my being alone and not being lonely after gaining a tremendous amount of wisdom. I did relationship recovery work and was able to move beyond all those heartaches and heartbreaks. I became the teacher who practiced what she taught to others.

There were times I would float in and out of dating. Luckily I had I had shifted from being needy to a spiritual desire to share divine love. After all my astrology chart said two marriages, one later in life so it had to be true right? I sat on the beach one day doing my meditation and asked if a divine complement was something I should even consider. I really wanted a sign. I kept saying, "Show me; show me; show me." About five minutes later I opened my eyes, and was just looking at the water and enjoying my day at the beach. A seagull arrived and dropped down right before me. In his beak he had a strand of pink beads kind of like those stretchy bracelets you wear as a bangle bracelet. He dropped the bracelet at my feet and flew away after nodding his head at me to look down.

"Holy cow," I thought, "is this my sign?" I washed off the bracelet in the ocean and put it on my right hand for my future and said "well I asked and you delivered". Pink is the color of joy and happiness. As strange as it sounds I got my sign dropped right at my feet that I might just want to consider sharing love once again.

I remember one evening sitting in my living room stretching to the Universe and saying,

"Thank you, I absolutely love love love my life! Thank you Universe. I am so in love with you and all you have given me. Thank you, thank you, thank you. I love me; I am enough; I am love; I am light; I am whole. Bliss bliss and more bliss. You know what Universe? I know I felt I wanted to share love, but I really love my life. I no longer have to try this dating game. I have no desire or want or need for anyone beyond myself. I accept that I will age without a life partner, and I am grateful to embrace this awareness."

I did not give up. I surrendered to a new viewpoint.

I was so happy that I no longer had to go on dates and explain myself. I wasn't disappointed. I wasn't even relieved. It just was what it was. There was no sadness or regret. I was just plain happy. I felt it was the end of a story. I was ready to put that book on the shelves of the eternal library and stamp it 'no longer necessary I have read everything'. I was actually thrilled thinking I am going to age gracefully doing the work I love. I am so blessed with where I live and who my friends were, playing tennis twice a week, writing and teaching, traveling and spending quality time with my sons. Not a bad life. Actually I felt it was a perfect life. I felt light joyful and really wanted or needed nothing. I had it all. I was peaceful. I wasn't rich, but I was wealthy in my soul. I was content. Everything fell into place easily and nothing was missing. I had a smile on my face from the minute I woke up in the morning to the last prayer of gratitude on my lips at night. I was in total acceptance in this state of being joyful. It lasted for about two weeks.

Then the Universe said, "Oh really? You thought you were done didn't you? Well guess what, you're not. We want you to share your state of being love with someone else.

You are a spiritual teacher. Have you forgotten that the Universe and God as its architect shares love through all creation? Love continues to grow through replication. You see this in nature all the time don't you? Why can't you see that you must continue to share your light all the time? I do share my light. I share it every single time the phone rings and someone needs me. That is not enough said the voice. Love must continue to grow at all times just like you. Your soul must continue to evolve to a greater state of wisdom as well. This is how it works; get over yourself."

I was so darn happy. Just so darn happy, I had surrendered to the art of loving and courting myself so purely that my life was exactly the way the Universe wanted. I had worked so hard to arrive at this place and then they take it away. Just like that. I guess the Universe is fickle. They are never satisfied. They wanted more. I thought I had given everything and then I realized once again this is another surrender to divine will.

Put your big girl panties on and buckle up sister. You got an email which you wanted to delete. You didn't understand how it even came through because you were done. Yet there it was. The subject said 'The Journey'. A person actually wrote that. My finger hung over the delete key, but I left it alone. I read it again. Hmmmm. Curious. Read it.

Only ten minutes away. Maybe. I am so darn happy; I am so darn happy; I am so darn happy. Do I have to answer this? Yes. Do it. Urgh.

Relationships are not for everyone, and if you have arrived at that place of surrender and acceptance of living a life without a partner without any regrets, then I bless you a million times. If you are fulfilled with family and friends that may be exactly what you signed up for in this lifetime. If you are living a life from a point of serving others and that fills your heart, you have fulfilled a huge part of your divine destiny. If you have left relationships in the past in an honorable place with conscious closure you may really be ready to embrace your singular life.

Consider giving love a second chance if you are in a relationship a marriage or even single and you do yearn for someone to share love with. Go back to the beginning if you are in a struggling relationship. Remember loving each other. You may have a lot of history with this person so consider the investment you already have in each other. Can that be revisited from a place of self awareness not to do damage control but soul control?

A second chance for me in sharing the lost art of loving through conscious courtship with my second husband was very scary. We broke up once for three months while engaged. We then gave our relationship a second chance to develop into a true partnership. The second chance came when we decided to try it again because truly we did love each other. We were good friends and companions. The one thing my husband said when we got back together was "we have to do it differently this time". He was right and that was what worked for us. A second chance at courtship requires a change of attitude and a change of habits. You have to be open to doing it differently.

The best advice anyone ever gave me was a friend from Sedona who also had a second marriage. She told me the first year of marriage was really hard for them. She discovered her secret solution was giving up the need to be right all the time. Wow, I thought this sounds so simple. The more I applied this the better things became. The perfectionist in me still needs to be applying this on a regular basis and here is how I do this. I do not agree with my husband on many things. He and I are not perfect. I do say the words "I understand" often. It merely means I hear what you are saying and I acknowledge that. It does not say however I agree with everything you are saying. Sometimes we just need to be heard.

My new husband showed me who he really was when I had my heart surgeries. He cooked all my meals, did all my laundry (well you know he loves doing laundry right?).

He cleaned my bathroom took me to my doctor's appointments, and he always asked me if I needed anything. Talk about appreciation. I could not have had two heart surgeries without that help. I learned to be more thoughtful. I had to change my habits and be okay with not being right all the time. Even though I would love to believe I am right, what is the point in making his opinions worthless? Nobody wins in that game of right/wrong polarity.

Tell the man you love what you appreciate about him. Tell the woman you love how special she is and why. It's a good start at second chances. When you put the needs of another before your own needs, you are in service to building love again merely for the sake of sharing your own divinity with another. You serve your soul and their soul at the same time in the sacred contract of connection which generates more contentment. There is something alchemical that happens when you put your own needs aside and attend to loving the needs of another as a form of service. You feel better and are open to receiving and giving more love.

I read an email once about a divorced man who made a list about marriage advice. The number one item he listed that stood out among many was never stop courting. He said he wished he had done things differently.

From the male perspective, I loved what he wrote: "When you asked her to marry you, you promised to be that man that would own her heart and to fiercely protect it. This is the most important and sacred treasure you will ever be entrusted with. Never get lazy in your love. " We all need to remember that. Never get lazy in how you court and love each other every day—no matter in what small way.

We spoke about the rose petals of the heart previously. Like these rose petals, love is layered. I had some friends who went on a vacation to Paris. They told me they fell in love again and at another level. It was so sweet to hear this. Love is not a stagnant thing.

It moves as an energy field of wholeness. When we share love with another, it has the ability to continue to grow in many ways and many directions. Courtship is continual.

It does not stop with marriage or divine complement. Try to really see the best in your partner. Remember to play and have fun. Life isn't all about serious stuff. Create a play date with each other and make it fun. Laugh at the stupid stuff. Forget your critical parent voice, that doesn't belong to a couple falling in love over and over again. Allow each other time with their friends because everyone needs a little space. I call it my 'me time'.

When I tell my husband, I need some ' me time ', I am going shopping alone, he just says okay have fun. Sometimes I go to my temple and meditate alone. It feels good to be alone with the Universe. I also spend time with my girlfriends. My husband balked at this when we first got married but then I showed him an article from a prominent university study on brain chemistry which he knows a lot about. The study showed that when women spend time with female friends the happiness they experience affects a hormone in the brain. The end result is you get a happier woman if you are not glued to her side all the time. Trust that she needs 'me time' big time!

My husband is also learning to ask for his own 'me time'. He is a big gym bum as he calls himself so the gym time, three times a week is his time. As partners you are not each others answer, you are your own answer. Hopefully as your love grows and expands for yourself it will continue in its own unique way to also grow with those you share love with. Do not compare yourself to other couples. Establish what works for you. Life is not supposed to be a competition. Regarding your intimate, 'we time' what is normal for you is just that, normal for you. Although you may read reports on studies that say, 'the average number of times per week to have sex is' , let it go. Do what works for both of you. Talk about it and let it be spontaneous. It is not a job. It is pleasure remember?

Be the Master of Your Mind and the Mistress of Your Soul

—Johanna Carroll

PART IV
LOVING IN THE NEW AGE

The Age of Enlightenment

The original Age of Enlightenment was also called the Age of Reason. This was a cultural movement of intellectuals beginning in late 17th and 18th century Europe. It emphasized reason and individualism rather than tradition. Its purpose was to reform_society using reason, to challenge ideas grounded in tradition and faith and to advance knowledge through the scientific method. It promoted scientific thought, skepticism and intellectual interchange.

We return once again to another Age of Enlightenment. The 1960's was a time of radical movement of extremes as an example of change in motion. Once again, the traditions of that time where challenged. However, rather than a purely intellectual movement this refined age is considered by many to be a spiritual movement of merging head and heart. It was the dawning of a new error where many dove into the pillow of their heart to discover their souls. It was a time of consciousness raising once again to discover the mysteries of life. It was an awakening to new spiritual beliefs beyond traditional religion.

Many people reached to the ancient ways of eastern philosophises tribal cultures and beyond the stars. The higher mind of thought merged with a greater desire to be reborn through awareness wisdom and love. The ending of the Age of Pisces and the dawning of a new era is referred to as the Age of Aquarius. These ages have a direct impact on the current Age of Enlightenment. We will discuss this in an upcoming chapter.

Mankind is moving toward a deeper consciousness on the planet. We are still bending and moving through the gateway to new thought as a continuum of the original Age of Enlightenment. We are once again redefining value systems that no longer apply to us personally. The mind altering drugs and free wheeling sex of the 1960's have been replaced with a healthier journey to consciousness raising. The search for individual freedom still continues in a new journey. This has become a personalized quest of the spiritual pilgrim yelling and screaming for a new way to feel whole and have their personal life make sense.

It is no mistake that you decided as a soul to be born in this age time and place. When you decided to take a life based on the desire for gathering information, you also made an agreement with your soul. You agreed that in signing up for life, or reincarnating, which means a return to the flesh, that the gathering of information also included learning lessons. You also agreed that in this age you were born into, you would take that knowledge that made you smart and continue to grow on the journey of life. You agreed as a soul that from the smart stuff you learned from life's lessons, not only would you be smart but you would do life differently in any choices you made. As I have stated before, there is a blessing in everything even in the negative yuck of life. That blessing is wisdom and what you learned about yourself. This is an age of self awareness and your life is the stage upon which you live out your divine plan. Those blessings also encourage you to remember how to court your own soul. You become the master of your mind in making choices and the mistress of your heart and soul in loving yourself fully.

When you do life differently based on what you learned from those life lessons, you are now applying wisdom. Wisdom comes from the soul. Wisdom is the application of an action activated by a desire for a better day and a better way of living from your heart and soul. It is generated by the higher mind or what is referred to as your superconscious self.

Your higher self is in charge, not your ego or limited lower mind that says you know it all. You are no longer full of yourself. You are full of the desire to fully love and be loved. You don't know it all yet you can improve on your life by taking what you have learned and turn things in a positive direction. You no longer go backwards, you move forward. You lift your feet out the mud of life and shift. You part the veils of illusion and delusion and get a glimpse of the divine that lives within you. There is a palpable gentle feeling each day that you are no longer stuck but moving forward. You apply the wisdom of self love and use your wisdom in sharing love with others no matter who they are; friends, family, extended family, your peers at work, or your love choices on an intimate level. You have learned through your mistakes that maybe you need to choose differently. The first choice you make is to love yourself without conditions. This is not an excuse for bad behavior it is a choice for living fully and serving your soul not your ego. Life becomes kind.

There are many teachings in religion, science and metaphysics that are relevant. I feel one of the most powerful ones for you to understand is how amazing you are as a spirit and a person is the understanding of these words enlightenment and energy we hear about all the time. I want to share this with you so you can see just how amazing your choice of life is. Maybe this will help you remember who you truly are as an instrument of love.

It all started with one sentence: *'Let there be Light'*. Whether you believe in the scientific theory of the big bang, God parting the clouds, or the Garden of Eden with this mantra of direction, light or energy was created. It has intelligence and it had a purpose.

We think of light as a field of illumination. God parted those clouds of the Universe, directed the flashlight of the Universe upon the cosmos and saw the intention of creation to share divine love through the illumination of all beings.

Let's take the phrase *'Let there be Light'* and interpret what light actually is: cosmic intelligence. What does it mean to you personally to share divine love filled with wisdom from above? Divine illumination is what happens when we open to the divine. It is how we light up our own soul to have that memory and connection that we are not just a human being. We desire to know and remember that we are so much more than a person living an automated life. We begin to trust at a deep level that by connecting to this greater self, we can find some semblance of balance, harmony and inner peace. We grasp the belief that the meaning of our life is more than the weekly paycheck and living a robotic lifestyle.

We actively search or long for the feeling of being connected to something far greater than ourselves. This is the quest to taste the divine. Some people often refer to this as the home they remember. "I want to go home." I hear that so often and the response is always the same. "What does home mean to you? What is the home you feel you are seeking, do you know? Is it a place, a person or a thing? Or is the memory of home a feeling that you can't describe but joy bubbles up every time you feel this way? Do you actively have a relationship with your soul? Do you know who you are as a human being? Do you know what serves your self and your soul? Are you okay with knowing this and honoring your boundaries?" These are the questions of the spiritual pilgrim.

The desire is to know ourselves as a human and divine being working in total partnership.

It is the concept of divine consciousness or intelligence seeking the home that their soul remembers. We feel we are separate from this divinity because we are after all mere mortals. Self awareness is self discovery. Traditionally many religions preach that God is outside of us floating somewhere up up and away in those heavenly clouds. The rules say if we follow this religion this God or that God this teaching or that then we will feel better. This may work for some but not all. The spiritual quest to experience the presence of the divine becomes the journey to return to the inner home.

The Age of Enlightenment now is a spiritual rebellion that appears to be gathering greater force and attention. It is the quest for who I am as a spirit, a soul that is not separate or outside of me. I become my own God / Goddess and merge totally as one light of illumination as a whole soul self. I seek enlightenment. I seek more illumination wisdom cosmic intelligence. There is a burning desire at a cellular level to remember who I am as a spiritual being. More than ever before many crave being illuminated or lit up as a soul.

We desire as a group of soul seekers to remember what our intuition has been telling me.

That tug on my heart that says 'there is more' does want to lighten up! Listen. Go within.

You will find enlightenment when you return to the home of your soul once again.

How many of you reading this at some point in time feel you became the spiritual rebel of your family? Were you the one saying "no there is more to life than being a robot."

I want more. I want to know my soul. Just the mere thought of those words opened the gates of time across the veils. You repeated the first words of all creation. "Let there be light in me. Let there be light within me lighting my own life path."

- You allow the flashlight of the Universe to reflect on your personal path of life.

- A cosmic intelligence shines from the inside out.

- You desire soul awareness at a very deep level that is private personal and unique for you.

- You begin to connect your body mind emotions and spirit.

- You know yourself as divine being who is eternal.

The word enlightenment simply means to become wiser. All light or intelligence exists within the mind. You are asking for the wisdom of the Universe in every thought word or deed. The quest of the spiritual seeker is to have a personal private relationship with the divine. It is a desire to remember that state of divinity we call love and live it each day.

The ego is there to keep you real and grounded in the human experience. It is not a bad thing to be in your ego. It is *how* you use your ego that will cast you up or down on this path of light. How do you call your soul to guide you? A soul call is a return to the source of all that is whether you refer to this as God Universe spirit, God / Goddess it does not matter. What matters is your relationship to this divine source that is full of love. How you make that concept real is how you expand love in order to reclaim infinite consciousness. We know we want to be loved. We believe we want to love each other as we love ourselves. How do you express this love personally is yet again another freewill choice. There are no boundaries on love as a state of being divine. It is endless and limitless just like the Universe.

In reaching your hand to your personal source of enlightenment, do you get the answers and guidance you are seeking? Are the answers clear so you can understand them?

Science tells us that in the 12 strands of DNA in each cell, a large portion is dedicated to a higher intelligence. A great confirmation that light does live inside of us. How can you merge with the divine that lives within every particle of your personal DNA? This is location in your body where you literally do light up by activating soul awareness.

We live in an exceptional and interesting time. We have been told that we are living in a time of huge change and energetic shifts. If you look around at the world right now, we all are wondering if the chaos is a precursor to something else of greater magnitude.

What if the chaos was part of a new way of living? What if a shift of cosmic energy patterns that affect everything in the Universe is also affecting you? Chaos is a precursor to change and change is often just what we need to evolve.

There are two constants in the world that were ignited by ' *Let there be Light*'. They are love and change. Love is the state of being divine and whole at all times. It is the vibrational matter you were created from. Love is not dependent on anything or anyone outside of you. You *are* love and like the song says all there is is love. It is divine matter.

Change carries the experience or the flow of life or divine vibration moving shifting and pushing us toward greater evolution. We agreed as human beings that we would have the experience of life to gather knowledge. We seek as a soul to apply that knowledge to move beyond limitations. We gain wisdom so the soul can evolve. How many times have you repeated the same experience again and again with the soul screaming in the background, "hey you, did you get it yet? This is not working and we would like you to change!" Relative to sharing love with others, you already know you have to start loving yourself a brand new way before you can receive it differently from others.

Many reject change. We fear change because we think it messes everything up. What if you shifted your perception of change as the flow of cosmic energy? What if you could have more wholeness divine bliss and a total state of love? Where have you tried to fight change only to accept it and then realize change was a gift? Like a river flowing gently through the Universe you float through life. You watch and embrace life for all it has shown you. Whether you consider it good or bad when the soul speaks you know within your heart that blessings come. It is up to you to see your life itself as the gift. It is a gift to know it is an honor to be alive. Right here, right now.

Here are some suggestions to take you to a deeper place of illuminating your soul for greater enlightenment:

- Realize you are not alone. You have the entire Universe with you including people on the earth you can align and merge with. Find your spiritual family and see how wonderful this support system is for you as inter-dependent pilgrims journeying on the same path. This can be a traditional religion or something that you once thought was alternative. Find what works for you and feels loving.

- The way it was is not the way it is now. Break your pattern of thinking and shift so you can open to new inspiration.

- Turn over to the Divine what you cannot handle. They can handle anything. You go for a walk. Give your mind a rest and stop over analyzing everything.

- To understand the matrix of the 'now' moment, realize clearly you are deceiving and stopping your process of soul evolution by attaching to the past or the future.

- This is a highly evolved Age of Enlightenment. It is the age of self sufficiency.

Let go of co-dependent behaviors and embrace change as a major gift for a better way of living.

- Unplug from life to feel the flow of the divine moving all around you. Sit still, change your day and allow for moments of quiet and silence, even if only for five minutes. Like a cloud of light you will start to feel lighter.

- Imagine a white circle of light all around you. Breathe into it. Now imagine it gets larger. Be quiet with this. Ask for what serves you now for the human you and the spiritual you. Wait. Be aware. Smile more.

The Age of Enlightenment is here in full throttle. The question for you is where do you wish to exist in this age? Only you can direct your own light. The first step is knowing it is there. Waiting for you to come home.

Intuition—Your Telephone Line to the Divine

You made an agreement in your sacred contract to have another life, to evolve and move beyond what had limited you in the past. The word intuition has almost become a common word used these days. Although in the past it was considered something connected with the world of the occult. We now know that your intuition is something to pay attention to yet often we push it aside like a pesky mosquito. We make intuitive decisions all the time and often they are unconscious. How do you use your intuition as a telephone line to the divine to activate your wisdom rather than the needs of your ego?

How many times have you repeated something from the past even though your intuition says, uh oh here we go! We ignore our intuition when it is trying to guide us to a better choice.

The body is a field of light and emotion. Our mind and our feelings are part of the journey that we tap into. You may have been told in terms of your job to leave your personal issues at the door to the office. How is that working for you? Can you really detach from what you are feeling if it is overwhelming you? This is very hard and almost impossible to do. You store it away and then when you walk out the door. You pick up from where you left off. Bravo to you if you can handle this. If you cannot, plug into your intuition and ask this question. "How can I store an excess of emotion to address later in the day?" Listen to what your higher mind says. If you feel you can't detach, give yourself permission to pray for a way. Trust that what you are feeling is the hand of the Universe on your heart giving you comfort.

How do you know if you can trust your intuition? I have had a lot of people tell me they have met someone new and just know intuitively that this is the perfect match for them. Then a month goes by and they are questioning what they thought was the voice of intuition guiding them and now it is a mistake.

There are two types of intuition; pure and warped. Information or light in the form of intuitive hits or thoughts come in three waves. I refer to this as the three waves of bliss.

Consider yourself a surfer on the sea of life. There you are sitting on your surfboard waiting for the next wave to carry you forward to shore, your future. How can you trust that voice of intuition if you get it wrong some of the time? Pure intuition comes like a whisper from eternity very gently and quickly. In the first three to ten seconds of a message, trust what you are feeling. The voice of intuition speaks in your high holy heart.

This is the heart that is sacred not scared. The first wave of bliss is a knowing clear as a bell. Consider this the first intuitive message.

If you are getting some kind of thought or feeling ask if there is more to that message.

Consider it the second part of the message, the second wave. Sit and wait. Be still.

Here is the last intuitive or telepathic message that you generate as a question " is there anything I need to do?" Wait. If you hear no then do nothing. If you see a red light, it means no. Your mind understands a red traffic light. If you see a green light it means yes move forward. Keep this dialogue with divinity simple and don't complicate it. Your brain will give you an intuitive message connected to something that is natural for you to understand hence the traffic signal colors of red and green representing no or yes.

If you need to ponder a life changing event, find time in nature because this is where we have the reflection of the Universe in everything. It is the garden of the soul so use it wisely. If you live in a city, bring something of nature into your home even if it is a rock.

Connect to this with your hands. Close your eyes and ask for guidance. Listen to your intuition so you can connect to the divine. Warped intuition comes from your ego. You will get a gentle nudge or message of knowing from the Universe that you didn't expect.

Your ego will start to edit the message. Now your mind is trying to control outcomes instead of allowing the voice of your telephone line to the divine to guide the way. Trust it, don't edit it.

You can use this spiritual tool for anything from interviewing for a new job making a choice of a new home or dating. Here is an example regarding dating someone you have never met. Before you even go into the neutral place you are meeting for the first time to have that glass of ice tea rather than a bottle of wine which will distort your intuition (just a genuine suggestion for all you daters out there) sit in your car for a few moments. Close your eyes and ask to be connected to the energy of the person you are meeting. Ask for a genuine connection and start to feel what is there. Ask your soul to guide you not your mind. What are you feeling, warm or cold? Ask for more to the message. If you get nothing, then go in and enjoy the day. Even then while you are visiting with this person drop the mental list. Try to feel if there really is a heart to heart connection that feels genuine. Don't edit or go into fantasy. See beyond the physical and connect with the soul of the person sitting in front of you. Your pure intuition will never fail you so trust it.

The Over-Soul

The sacred teachings of the ages refer to the Over-Soul in many various ways. In the Bhagavad Gita, one of the most profound spiritual works I have ever read, the reference to the Over-Soul is a conversation between the voice of the divine and humanity. "Never was there a time when I did not exist." The voice of divinity further explains itself by referring to the "unchanging Over-Soul of God."

Let me give you a visual about your soul. The soul is eternal and you already know that.

It never dies. When that first spark of desire to experience life began your soul was born.

For each lifetime that your soul experienced, you gathered a pearl of wisdom. The pearl is not what you learned about others. It is what you learned about yourself. As your soul evolved through the ages and lifetimes, for each pearl of wisdom you strung it on the silken cord of experience. This connects you to the Universe. Like a luscious string of precious pearls each lifetime stretches out before you. You have access to all those memories of wisdom. They exist as soul memory in your Over-Soul.

We have heard so often this saying of body mind and spirit. Hopefully by now you realize that if you live your life purely from the physical body you are setting up a foundation for failure. I feel personally that this needs to be rewritten to say spirit mind emotion and then body. If you build your life from a spiritual place first, you have created an amazing foundation that is solid and clear in divine will and intention. This is why in all relationships friendship that is built from the soul plane of awareness has a greater depth. It is fed by eternal wisdom. Sophocles said that "Wisdom is the supreme part of happiness." The Dalai Lama has said "We cannot grow spiritually unless we are happy."

Metaphysics is a combination of science, psychology and spirituality. Science has many new advances on the relationship of brain chemistry and the effects of your emotional happiness on the health of the body. I could blame my genetics for my heart almost failing but no one in my birth family had heart disease. I really feel that my emotional heartbreaks over the years had a huge impact. You know when your heart is breaking emotionally because you feel pain. It is real it is valid and it needs attention. You really do have heartache. Any doctor that tells you that all you need to do is swallow a pill to make you happy is wrong because the pill is not enough. Although the medicine can calm things down which is wonderful it does not touch the core issues.

The good news is that in medicine today I feel there is a new model of attaining better mental health and physical well being. In this integrative concept paying attention to the voice of intuition is being recognized as valuable. My intuition kept telling me I had something wrong with my heart. Why didn't I listen to that? I should have insisted when I just resisted.

The main body we need to first pay attention to i
body as a field of energy.

You have a whirling swirling emanation of light or divine
conscious Over-Soul that flows all around you. This energy, the
totality of your soul, is a magnetic field of electric energy. It is
reflecting as light as intelligence that is soul generated from the divine
plan.

Your soul made a decision to experience life again and to
continually exist within the four primary realms or planes of
awareness. They are the spiritual, mental, emotional and physical
realms or simply put spirit, mind, feelings and body. Each one is
concurrent with the other. Although they have separate intention,
they are part of the whole design of your humanity and how you live
your life. It is so beneficial to understand how you personally walk in
and out of each realm. Your life will show you the results of the
influence of the Over-Soul in all four realms.

The spiritual plane of awareness is where our divine plan or
contract is initiated through the world of spirit. People, events,
situations, opportunities and sometimes challenges are created
through the intention of your reincarnation contract. These people,
events, situations, opportunities and challenges are created as
experience. You signed up for them when you co-created your
contract. Many times we included people from a past life to show up
once again so we could balance out our karma with them and
complete the unfinished business. That was a collective agreement.
We once again have experience with these people so both parties can
grow, gain knowledge and wisdom and evolve in soul consciousness.

What should matter to you in this current age of self-reliance is your commitment to do that work for yourself. It is your job to take care of you, to be aware and 'get it'. It is not your job to heal the rest of the world. Your job is to heal yourself first. Your job is to take care of yourself and not expect the world or anyone else to do that. You agreed spiritually to live as an independent soul not a needy soul. You will heal yourself by knowing yourself. When you discover the God-spark within you, you will see all the forces that are connected throughout the entire Universe. By doing this the world gains the benefit of your healing. You are part of a whole but you are not insignificant in any way. This is part of Universal law. In the spiritual plane of awareness, your only job is to be aware of who and what is presented as experience as an opportunity for growth.

In the mental plane of awareness the mind begins to create what is known as thought forms around the people, events, situations, opportunities or challenges directed by the spiritual plane. In other words, the mind puts forth a thought around what the spirit has placed before us as experience. The mind can be the trickster that is for sure and it is often said that the mind is the devil's playground. Delusion and illusion is the playground of the lower energies often called the Satan. In traditional religious teachings, this is a heavy low field of energy. It is pure fear.

The mind is the place where your ego, intelligence, reasoning self and beliefs as an imprint of information exist. This is where we start to think about what spirit has placed before us as experience. So a picture begins to be created in the mind of what this experience will look like. The gatekeeper to the doorway of higher consciousness is the ego which we have reviewed before. The ego has a purpose which is to keep us grounded in the body. Without the ego, why would we need a body in the first place? We would only be pure spirit and that is not what we signed up for.

There is a dualistic aspect that first shows up in the mind. It is through the Law of Polarity that all energy takes form. The Law of Polarity simply is that opposites of all energy exist in the world of form. Here you are with a new person who shows up in your life. You start to think about that person. You have a positive thought about them or perhaps you have a negative thought about them. They both could be valid thoughts.

Who knows until you have the experience right? The Law of Polarity is here to assist you in your awareness and to give you greater understanding and awareness. If you are coming from a spiritual perspective of awareness and not judgment you will begin to see that everyone who shows up in your life has something to give you in terms of experience. They are not here to teach you anything about yourself. You are here to learn about yourself through the relationship with them.

The experience with this person is intended to provide a platform for your growth as a person. It is merely an opportunity that has many gifts included in it. Specifically you are learning more about yourself (knowledge) applying that knowledge (wisdom) and evolving as a soul (evolution and ascension) from having the experience with this person. The important key to remember is that each person who shows up in your life is an opportunity for more self-realized awareness. Through that person you can learn more about yourself and gain tremendous benefits. I believe that there is a gift in everything and everyone. That gift is answering the eternal question, "who am I?" The mind can open the gateway to wonderful self-learning or can hold you back.

Think of your mind in a dualistic manner like the blade of a sword. On one side of the sword (your thoughts and ideas) are positive. Your thoughts are positive and are empowering. They protect you. Your thoughts that are negative can cause pain. The mind therefore is a place of great power or pain based on your thinking. This is a good time to take a few minutes and ask yourself these questions:

- Check your thinking. Do you generally think about what is wrong with a person or do you think about what is right with that person?

- Change your thoughts and the whole world changes around you. Are you focusing on what isn't there or what is there?

- Do you come from a place of lack or a place of abundance?

- Do you think from fear or do you think from love?

- How can you begin to think thoughts from a positive place rather than negative?

You may want to put the book down and review these questions as a form of processing a new perspective. Ask yourself these questions listed above and take a little time to ponder this.

- Are my thoughts moving me ahead in life or holding me back? Pick a particular person in your life right now. List your positive thoughts about this person, Now list your negative thoughts.

Take a few minutes and get quiet. Reviewing the positive and the negative together as a whole experience, what do you think the gift of having this person in your life is or was? Remember we learn as much from the negative as we do from the positive. Take each one and go back and review what it is that you would like to learn about yourself from the experience to have a greater awareness. What did this person teach you about yourself? List all the items and start to see the results or the gift you got just from knowing them. Give this some time and attention. You might be surprised what you will learn about yourself. Do you think your thoughts on this person have now changed based on new awareness? See how powerful your thoughts are? "I think; therefore, I am" is very close to the truth of it all.

The emotional plane of awareness is where the feeling state of consciousness exits. This is where we begin to put an emotion to our thought around the experience that has been presented. The Earth is the planet for an emotional warehouse. We are very emotional creatures. Sometimes we let our feelings run our lives instead of the whole personality engaging in complete awareness. If we combine a negative thought with negative emotions, we are like a bomb ready to explode. However, if we use discernment and positive emotions around positive thoughts we can be in pure bliss. Now wouldn't that be a sweet way to walk through life?

When we are in the emotional plane of awareness we combine the feeling state with thought. We begin to formulate an opinion based on emotion. That emotion can be love happiness acceptance and understanding or can run the entire range of the emotional roller coaster which can create confusion in decision making. The emotional plane of awareness is where freewill shows up and makes a decision to say either, "Yes I will have this experience," or "No I will not have this experience based on how I feel about it." The emotional plane of awareness is also the home of your intuition. Intuition generally comes first as a feeling or a sense of something. It is important to honor that pure intuition and ignore the warped intuition of the ego which can lead you astray to bad decisions.

The emotional plane of awareness is the crossroad point where the spirit the mind and the emotions join together and make decisions. This is called the crossroad point because you can go in either direction. When we join the spiritual mental and emotional planes of awareness together we move beyond the cross road point of decision making based on freewill. We now are in the physical plane of awareness also called the garden of manifestation. This can be a heavenly garden or it can be rather hellish.

The physical plane is actually the world you live in. It is where the results of the three other planes manifest or create a physical event or experience to occur. Mind and matter become one. Our inner planes of spirit mind and feelings have created something to occur in our outer or physical world. It is the material world of people possessions money. The heavenly garden is filled with joy and happiness. This what 'living heaven on Earth' means. It is also the place we get to work out our karma and create a new way of living.

Instead of surviving and suffering we begin to thrive with the awareness of our own divinity. In the alchemy of the magnetic fields of awareness that we live in we float like feathers on waves of light. It is not divinely intended by your soul that you feel trapped into a body that is imperfect. Your life is not a big cosmic joke where you were duped into living a life that is heavy. There really is an amazing opportunity to feel like that feather; completely free. Love ascends beyond the physical realm to something far greater and joyful when devotion exists to wholeness of loving and understanding yourself first. You never feel trapped.

Heart Strings

In reflecting and projecting your inner light onto another and receiving it returned, like a mirror, something magical exists in the flow of love in those waves of light between you. There is a dedication and devotion to the art of loving. This creates the magnetic movement of sharing the light of your own devoted heart and soul to replicate divine love. You become an instrument of the Universe. This wave of light that moves between two people I have often referred to as a heart string because this is exactly what it looks like to me; a string of light. A heart string is an energetic connection. It is a field of light known as cosmic intelligence that moves between two people. Imagine a bright yellow piece of yarn and that you have a big magnifying glass in your hands. See how those little fibers of yarn extend up and seem to be moving in the wind? Now imagine that all around and inside that piece of yarn is electricity moving back and forth connecting two hearts together. Feel it? It feels warm alive and vibrant. It never stops moving. Even if someone is sad the heart string is still connected. It is a divine connection of one heart to another. One soul remembering the soul of another.

Love that is divinely intended is always present. We may be mad at someone. We may not like that someone. Underneath it all love is still there connected moving back and forth. It is a constant spiritual connection of each soul to the other. It is the light of divine love or an emergence of the higher intelligence of the Universal presence that wakes up the dormant God Code within. Love becomes the omnipresent river flowing through this heart string that connects you to the sacred heart of another. This is sharing love as an art form of the living Universal presence. You as a person and you as a couple become united with one purpose which is to share your divine selves.

Kathy?.?.

Piscean and Aquarian Ages

We live in very interesting times as human beings. There has been a whole shift that you can almost feel like the ground rolling under your feet moving you towards something new. For many people, it creates restlessness and a quest for something perceived as better. There have been many teachings and a great deal of thought put into what is referred to as the Age of Aquarius. No one seems to really know or agree when the Aquarian Age began and there are many theories on dates. What is agreed upon in positive reflection is that this new age created shifts in group consciousness. This change of thinking also affects the way people behave. This would also affect your beliefs whether personal or religious social economic or political. Within all ages where a great social shift occurs, there is generally some kind of rebellion against the old form and it is usually radical in nature. We reject the old and embrace the new. The pendulum swings in an extreme to create cause and effect and change begins. Prior to the Age of Aquarius, we had the Age of Pisces. The Piscean Age once again cannot be captured in a date sequence because once again metaphysical historians never seem to agree on a date.

The symbol of the fish was used frequently in the early days of Christianity and is often also attributed to the Age of Pisces. It was during the Age of Pisces that Jesus turned the world upside down with what was known as radical thought. His teachings like those of all great masters are Universal. He came to teach the world love and kindness through brotherhood.

As in all ages, there are certain beliefs that capture how we respond to life in general.

The role of the soul is to continue to add to the string of the personal pearls of reincarnation to have a life to grow as a person and evolve as a soul. Sometimes a soul will have lived in the age preceding the one they are born in. Along with their birth in a new body they can carry forth some of that old karma to be revisited and refined. This is in the form of all personal relationships your religious beliefs economic status, etc. Each age has unique qualities. The Piscean Age has been referred to by some teachers as the age of the victim. Religious freedoms were at peril and to practice certain religions could have you crucified.

The Spanish Inquisition, in the name of God, decided they would cast out the demons and we know how hypocritical and how well that worked out. There was a lot of suffering.

People had limited choices and if they had what we would refer to now as their 'voice', life was not such a happy place for them. This age had limitations restrictions and a lot of rules. If you didn't play by their rules, you were doomed. The characteristics that belonged to the Piscean Age were fear, hate, revenge, envy, greed, jealousy, anger, rage etc. I think you get the picture. It was filled with intense heavy energy where fear lurked around every corner.

The Age of Aquarius, if you are old enough to remember the play Hair, was the dawning of something new. It was radical in nature. In this new age teachings or thought are sacred spiritual teachings taught in the mystery schools of higher intelligence before humanity descended fully into a fear based way of life. This age is an age of renewal and validation of what the soul already innately knows. We are a spiritual being having a human experience. I am sure you have heard that a million times and it is true. The characteristics of the Age of Aquarius are love based. They are awareness compassion and understanding. There is a desire to be happy and to change the old way.

In the 1960's, which was a rebellious age, one of the mottoes was make love, not war.

It was the introduction of the birth control pill and sex was rocking and rolling all over the place. Love compassion understanding awareness and community service created an awakening in the consciousness of mankind. Not everyone embraced the Aquarian Age. In fact many people still do exist in the Age of Pisces based on how they live their life. The good news is that now in this moment you have a choice. It is a choice of consciousness. This is the great shift that we hear so much about. I personally feel that we all have the opportunity to embrace a spiritual revolution which is the desire for a better way ignited by our soul. It is a desire to live from that place that is natural to the soul. A garden of peace bliss and happiness.

How does this relate to you and a return to the lost art of loving? How does this impact you on a personal level in conscious courtship? I hope this helps. If you or anyone else you know are living from a viewpoint of fear anger hatred revenge jealousy or greed, you or they are stuck in the Piscean Age and you will suffer. You create the suffering. If you are in an abusive relationship whether it is physical emotional mental or financial you are stuck in Piscean Age mentality.

If you are of the younger generation and entering the world of dating please pay attention.

In the Tibetan teachings addictions are referred to as the poisons. Addictions of any kind are poisons to the soul. This is addiction to food sex or drugs. Anything that is excessive places your heart and your soul in a pathway of suffering. You have a choice. Please remember that. You have a choice to be a spiritual rebel in your own group of friends and say "no." I know it isn't easy. I know you want to fit in. It isn't worth it in the long run.

Perhaps its time to review old habits to get wisdom on how to live today in this Age of Aquarius. This will affect your future.

The Age of Aquarius has gifted all of us with an incredible opportunity to do life differently and live from our heart and soul that is pure. I am suggesting you be selective in your choices. Not every person in the world is able to make choices. Not every person has the ability to control their situation. They do however have the ability to control their own soul as do you. The basis of the difference between the Age of Pisces and the Age of Aquarius is simple. You live from a choice of love or fear. When you walk in the shadow of divine love, you are waiting for the light of your soul to awaken the memory of oneness. This is the best drug.

Fear separates us from our soul. Love connects us to our soul. If you really desire to live from a place of happiness allow fear to disappear. Your mind is the center of your ability to create a consciousness shift. This is the basis for the Aquarian Age. Face your fears and replace them with love. Create a pathway that works for you.

I was raised in a traditional Catholic family in Connecticut. I started to have a connection with the divine at a very young age. I did not really understand what was happening until I was in my twenties. I did not reject my religion but it didn't feel that it was the right fit anymore. I explored other teachings and found a path that works for me. My relationship to God and the world of spirit is very personal as is yours. Mother Theresa was once asked about her religion. This is what she said: "I love all religions but I am *in* love with my religion."

Your life each day is your church and temple. The way you interact with people is how you live your spiritual teachings. Live from a place of goodness. Spend time in nature.

Find a connection to the higher power that is greater than you are. I feel humanity suffers now because we have forgotten our soul and are still living in the Piscean Age. It is not necessary to suffer any more remember that. If you are in any kind of relationship where you are suffering you do have a choice. All the great masters who lived on the earth were here to teach us something. Now you have the ability to be your own master and live from a viewpoint of your own soul leading the way. Not your ego or your mind but your soul. It takes dedication and determination to change your life. It begins with spiritual desire for a better way one thought and one step at a time. The future of the world needs your heart to be open kind and loving.

Age of Ascension

We are not trapped in a certain age and told we have to live a certain way. Each age has a cycle and energy that moves each soul within that cycle. Many people held their breath when they thought the end of the Mayan calendar was the end of the world. In every age there is an extreme that heralds the end of the world. I feel personally the end of the Mayan calendar was the doorway to a new consciousness shift to even greater enlightenment. Doomsday predictions generate fear. They keep you trapped in the Piscean Age.

Some people thought that in the Age of Ascension and the end of the Mayan calendar they would be lifted out of their bodies and taken off the earth to live in the divine realms. There was preaching about the end of times and if you were on an advanced path you would ascend in the blink of an eye. No one would know where you were or where you had gone but you would ascend spirit mind and body. The whole enchilada.

I sometimes wonder about this. How does this really help people live in the moment knowing that life is a divine playground not something to exit as quickly as possible? It does not feel spiritual to me. Anything that teaches fear push it away and trust what your heart and soul is telling you. When you do this understand your inner nature and awaken the god / goddess within. Once again you are the master of your mind and the mistress of your soul. If you are "what's in it for me" you are not in your divine nature. What belongs to you belongs to the world.

Another example for you to ponder regarding the shifts within the ages is the Hindu teachings of cycles. These cycles are called yugas. Within each cycle there are spirals of energy that move. One part of the cycles is an ascending cycle and one is descending.

Once again scholars do not agree on the timing of these cycles or ages but they do agree on one thing. Yugas are world cycles. Mankind lives in a history of cycles and ages.

Consciousness is rising and we no longer live in the dark ages. Some say we are in the Kali yuga. Others say we are in the Dwarpa yuga or age. Kali is the descending energy of destruction. Dwarpa is the ascending cycle of a higher state of wholeness. I feel they possibly exist together.

In the ascending cycle we see many advances in technology. We also see that technology can create war. In this regard, I feel we see evidence of the two cycles at play with each other. One thing I do know is this. We are no longer asleep. We are living in an Age of Ascension. Our soul has awoken. We are rising to soul awareness and have a desire to live from a personal space and place of contentment. You do have a choice to drop down into fear or rise up into the state of love. You have a choice to return to the lost art of loving your own soul first. You have freewill to make that choice. Even if you are trapped in a situation that seems ungodly, your mind and soul belongs only to you. No one can ever own your soul.

The Age of Ascension brings us many gifts and always we return to the inner journey of awareness as a pathway to ascension. I also believe there is an Ascension of Courtship.

This emotional and spiritual ascension in partnership, soul with self, gives freedom from surviving to thriving in a relationship. Your thoughts feelings and actions including your prayers are instructions to the Universe. Everything is energy and everything is a message that is delivered to the heart of the source of all life. Take one moment in time and surrender to a new way of thinking and being. Allow yourself to adjust and ascend.

Lately many friends and colleagues are reporting sudden deaths of clients and friends. I guess I could put myself in that category walking around waiting to have a major heart attack. I had sprained my hand and was unable to play tennis which I did faithfully twice a week. I felt it was divinely guided because if I had played tennis I probably would have died on the tennis court. I returned to tennis three months after my surgeries. I decided to join a small local tournament to get back in the game. I met an older man on the courts who wasn't feeling well but decided to keep on playing. We all told him to stop. Then I hear this scream from the court next to me, "Call 911." I had my nitroglycerin tablets with me and told one of the gals to put it under his tongue. It did nothing. He went into full cardiac failure on the tennis courts and died. It was shocking to see something like this. I could actually see the life force leave him which was an amazing thing to witness.

I felt I observed his ascension. At that point, I realized how blessed and lucky I was and as always felt very protected. My ascension had to wait. It wasn't my time to leave the planet.

Here is my viewpoint about the Age of Ascension. Ascension is a state of rising up beyond limitations. Some religious teachings call this resurrection. It is beyond balance.

It is wholeness. Wholeness occurs simply when you view the two poles of love and fear as each having value which leads you to greater awareness and understanding. Neither one is better than the other. They become equal teachers of wisdom on a personal level.

When you face your fears head on they no longer have power or dominion over you. You become a fearless spirit on a path ascending daily. You rise up to a higher state of living from the super consciousness of your spiritual higher mind rather than the limitations of the lower restrictions of the mind or the ego. Your mind becomes your friend not your foe. It does not matter if you are alone or with someone. What matters in the Ascension of Courtship is to know your divine destiny is your spiritual inheritance of love fully lived.

When you have achieved a state of ascension you have resurrected or rescued yourself from bad habits negative thinking and anything generated by fear greed jealousy anger or disappointment. You know the list. You have courted your soul to remember what the state of love is at all times. This is ascension. Ascension is the advanced state of courting the soul to marry the self. You become partners with your divine spirit and feel whole connected and one. The state of ascension connects at all times with the energetic harmonics or fields of light and love. This is connection with divine Universal wisdom and the state of pure bliss. We allow through our intention to exist reside and vibrate in this state while living an active life. The lessons have been learned, no repetition is necessary to have the same experience again and again.

When we gain and apply knowledge from a lesson we have learned and do life differently a shift occurs in the sacred mystery schools here on Earth known as life. The Universe says, "Hey guess what! No more need for that lesson to occur; they got it!" What you got was wisdom. The individual person learns from the lesson and gains knowledge. When they use that knowledge and react and behave differently even if only in their thinking the great cosmic shift occurs. You feel lighter you are happiness itself and you feel free.

Instead of being in school like a child learning lesson after lesson and repeating these lessons again and again, you have graduated. You have your PhD from the Universe.

Others learn through observing your actions and you have ascended. You are free from energetic burdens that the mind and body held onto sometimes for lifetimes. What a relief this is to feel and know you have arrived. Life joyfully begins to reveal some profound wisdom to you.

Now what you might ask does this have to do with igniting the lost art of loving and courtship? Everything. The first step of renewing the lost art of loving is to court your self. To thine own self be true, the master of your own destiny, the captain of your ship.

Courtship as a form of wooing and encouraging your own soul's desire for joy, peace and happiness must be initiated within yourself first. Call it forth, give it permission to be born, scream at the heavens if you will because you deserve to remember the full state of love from a tender loving fulfilled heart. Through this activation the memory of the home of the heart swells like a golden cup filled with the sweet taste of hope for a new life satisfied. This art form of loving and courting your own soul first sets in motion the magnetics of the Law of Attraction. The soul calls forth its choice of divine complement waiting to be discovered. Whether you respond to the result of that soul call is up to.

The New Temple of Learning

Your data bank of experience gives you the tools to build and create a new life. It is like building a temple made of three sides. This temple is a pyramid of power loaded with passion and a geometric form which looks like a triangle. It is a sacred geometric form.

Notice I did not say 'having' a relationship. I said "creating". Creating from the desire of spirit. The top of the triangle is God spirit the Universe whatever words work for you. It is the reflection of the higher intelligence that holds all divine power. It has the intention to share love and return all beings to the natural state of the soul; bliss. It holds the gateway to the Akashic records or book of life and all the wisdom your soul will ever need. It is the sacred source of all love. Love as the noun the state of being. Not the verb.

Consider that you are on the bottom side of the triangle. Another person is on the other side of the bottom of the triangle. If you desire to share the state of love fully with another and ignite those heartstrings from one heart to the other, each of you must go first to the top of the triangle then down to the other person. It is a pathway of gathering and then sharing love. You gather the greater wisdom of all divinity first. You draw it to yourself. You open your heart to share. You reflect this light of love to the other person.

They likewise go first to the top of the triangle to the source of all love and then draw that power to themselves. Just like you they reflect and project this light of love. The energy of the triangle is always moving. Love begetting love starts with the soul's desire first.

This is the foundation of creating a relationship that has some depth and meaning beyond the physical realm.

Guess what? This temple of wisdom has a name you know very well. It is called relationships. This temple is not exclusive. It includes every single being who crosses your path whether they seem significant or insignificant. Each soul that enters your life, even for a moment, is still an opportunity for you to learn about yourself. How we enter and exit that temple is up to you. We chose to interact with people beyond our own existence and through that exchange we open the doorway to self discovery. The journey of life continues through this temple system of learning every single day. It should be a journey of joy and welcomed for the advancement of your soul. Sometimes it doesn't feel like something we would have even chosen, but you did.

Wouldn't it be easier to just go live in the mountains all alone or climb into a cave to escape? In the ancient ages this is what many soul seekers for greater truths did. That was then and not now. We agreed when we chose this age of Aquarius to live in that we would be "in the world, but not *of* the world". We agreed we would actively participate in life for our growth and evolution. The desire to detach from the world has huge benefits.

We disconnect so we can connect. This is what retreat time is for; to disconnect from the world regroup energize your soul mind and body and get ready for more. We do this when we go on vacations an actual spiritual retreat or when we pray even for a moment.

Women do this when they meet friends for lunch or do a girls trip or personal 'me' day.

Men do this when they hang out with the guys in their man cave or golf vacations.

We need this time to move beyond an automated life into a life that is kind to the mind.

Our minds are on overload. If you could see the wiring in your brain, you would see that those wires are often just about ready to fry themselves fondly referred to as burn out. Burn out is a result of over stimulation and too much stress that needs a release big time. How often do you eat at your desk instead of taking a lunch and maybe going for a short walk to calms things down? How many hours is your mind plugged into something electronic? When does your body get some attention to relieve stress? Are you eating consciously instead of going to fast food which is exactly what it is. Food that is fast with no nutritional value? When do you sit and do nothing other than sleep? When you disconnect from the world and your normal way of day to day living, even for a short period of time, you plug into your soul if your intention is to get that rest and relaxation for your heart and soul. It is time to remember why you are here in the first place, not just to survive but to joyfully thrive.

Try this as a first step. No matter where you are (other than driving a car) at 9AM, 12PM, 3PM, and 6PM for one tiny moment, close your eyes take a breath and say thank you. That is all. Just thank you. If you can, get up and walk around for a minute. Look out a window a picture or anything that is beautiful to you. Just be still and be thankful.

If you can start to do this, you are giving your mind and body a mini minute retreat. That small action of disconnecting will eventually have positive effects if you are consistent.

Try it for a few weeks and then see if something in your life has shifted. Four times a day for one minute is four minutes a day. Out of 24 hours I am sure you can find 4 minutes a day for your heart and soul can't you? Each time you do this you enter an even greater temple of learning. It is the inner temple of your relationship with the divine that walks you to the door of your heart and soul.

Someone gave me these little sticky notes a few years ago. The saying that was written on them was pretty funny. "I meditate; I drink green tea, and I still want to slap someone." Maybe you feel you have done all your work as a spiritual pilgrim and life still whacks you in the head. Our lessons from the temple of learning never stop that is the point. Life will always show up. How do we manage those lessons in a new way so we don't get caught off guard? How do we stay balanced?

The catch word for a long time was balance. It still is something we try to understand on a personal level in the new temple of learning. How do I live a balanced life? What gives me balance? How do I use healthy boundaries to create balance? What are my boundaries? I know many people have done terrific work in understanding this. Is it really necessary to keep repeating the same situational experience so that you can learn that lesson again? Not in the Age of Ascension or the new temple of learning. As an evolved soul we have courted our own alignment with our spirit mind feelings and body.

We understand divine destiny. We are not better than anyone else and we have done our work. We live from a unified state of love, compassion awareness and understanding.

We have a relationship with the Universe unique in just the way that works for us. We know when a fear shows up how to find the gift of awareness in why it showed up in the first place. We go deeper for answers and insights. We pray we meditate we eat chocolate we call our friends. The golf game improves. You have a new respect for yourself and everyone you work with. Life is pretty darn good because we seek wisdom that is heaven bound. You have woken up spiritually and life in general is pretty nice.

If you feel the push pull of the world get clear on what brings you back to center. The center point I am referring to is your ability to live from spiritual wisdom you already know. Maybe you forgot and need to go back to the beginning. What I do know about this is that when you have a spiritual goody bag to reach into, you regain your balance.

Keep a list of three important spiritual teachings that return you to your heart. The moment something or someone pulls you off center go there. You may even be the cause of your imbalance. Start with this. Try to be true to the three principles of inner wisdom that feel real and ring true for you so you can come home to the temple within.

You can rise up from the polarity of love and fear into divine wholeness. This moves you beyond balance because you view everything as one source of wisdom. This is the goal of the soul living in this age and what I refer to as soul evolution. When you view life from the perspective that fear and love are great teachers where you learn so much about yourself, you know you gain wisdom. This is the state of unity or wholeness that has been also called 'agape'. Agape is a Greek word meaning love. This is the state of ascended or advanced love we have talked about before or love that is unconditional.

Agape is love which is of and from God whose very nature is love itself. Agape does not come from a source; it is the inner dweller source that illuminates the inner temple of relationships.

Although you may feel like the angel of love tossing love dust on every soul you meet, are you living your life in wholeness? Wholeness means you are never separated from the source of all creation, divine love. It means you have learned to navigate your life without those horrific dramatic emotional extremes. You have moved beyond knowing what keeps you balanced into knowing what keeps you whole. Definitely something to ponder as a human fragile soul.

Universal Teachings for the Single Soul

I hope at this point you will agree or even consider that the totality of your spirit mind feelings and body is a force of nature. It is filled with energy or spiritual prana also called the life force. Let the force of the source be with you. Just think of yourself like a giant light bulb waiting to illuminate. Perhaps you are already lit up all the time. I would like to think so. You love your single life and absolutely nothing is missing. As a matter of fact the thought of dating and having to explain yourself to a total stranger makes you ill.

Your life is working really well thank you very much without anyone else to share it with. You love your life and it is perfect. You understand how to negotiate life through the extremes to discover your own inner Universe of harmony. You understand balance.

You are clear on personal boundaries. You have had consciousness shifts and have embraced thinking about your life in a new way each day. You have put on your spiritual glasses and see life differently. You pray meditate eat consciously and spend time in nature. You connect with something far greater than you as a person and life opens doorways to the divine state of agape. You are having a love affair with the divine mystic that dwells inside of you. Life is serving you as you are serving it. You have purpose.

You have passion. You connect with the presence. You have created a home that feels like your personal temple. Your career has purpose.

You would love to be fully content and although you understand the concept of personal wholeness there is a little glitch in the Universal system supporting your life. You feel fulfilled don't you? So why are you perhaps still stuck? What is not moving? Do you have heartache and if so what needs to be healed? Is it time for a walk and talk with your soul to renegotiate that divine contract? Great. Just when you thought you had won the lottery prize in understanding fully the game of life, something or someone gets in the way and stops you in your tracks. What happened to my perfect life Universe? Are you playing cosmic games with me again?

I know of many single women in particular who think that time is running out for marriage and children. I was actually quite surprised in this Aquarian Age we live in that this would still be an issue. Yet many of my clients are in their 30's and 40's and feel there is a pressure from the world that something is wrong with them if they are not married.

Let me tell you a funny story about something that happened to me when I moved to Sedona, Arizona a number of years ago. I have been playing tennis for almost 60 years.

I love this sport so whenever I go anywhere I always look for the tennis courts. I had purchased a home in Sedona that was across the street from a resort that also had tennis courts which was perfect for me. I found out that every Saturday morning there was a group of mixed doubles so I decided that this would a great way to meet tennis players in the area. People were gathered on the side patio next to the courts waiting to find out who they would be playing with. A woman came up to me and I swear this is exactly what she said, "who do you belong to"? It kind of jolted me and after a moment I said, "I belong to God." She looked at me and continued to press me by saying, "No, seriously, who do you belong to?" " Oh", I said, "you mean am I married? No I am here by myself. I am single." She then patted my hand and said, "Don't worry dear; you will find someone." How odd she thought that because I was happily single and just wanted a good game of tennis!

I have thousands of clients who are female and have told me repeatedly this story about how they feel the world thinks something is wrong with them if they are not married or in a relationship. I find this really shocking that as a participant in the women's movement in the 1960's we still have not come a long way baby regarding this viewpoint. I just want to speak to any of you who feel this way. Here are some reminders:

- You are a beautiful soul no matter who you are with.

- Not every person is supposed to be married.

- In the joy of knowing yourself be honest. In courting your own heart and desires of the soul, if marriage is not your goal then own it.

If you are reading this book and you have family asking you all the time "when are you going to settle down" highlight this page and have them read it. I challenge you to do this if you feel being married is not the be all and end all for you. I would rather see any child of mine with wonderful friends and happy then getting married just for the sake of being married. Marriage and relationships should be based on the personal desire of each soul.

If you do want marriage make sure you want this for the right reasons, not because someone else is telling you there is something wrong with you because you are single.

Believe me being single has lots of wonderful advantages as does marriage and committed relationships. The grass is not greener on either side of the fence so stop the comparisons. It is a personal choice that should be honored and not questioned. Live your life for yourself and your soul satisfaction. You weren't born with anything missing and this idea of finding a perfect match just isn't realistic. If you want to consider dating then do it consciously. If you continually wish your life could be different based on someone else's standard you could be courting fear and sadness not faith and love in yourself.

A single life that is dedicated to a greater cause of personal fulfillment has its place on the earth. I don't mean you have to join a convent or sacrifice your entire life. A conscious choice of devotion to a career path with a profound mission of philanthropy and serving the world, even at some community level, is a great source of devotion and dedication. This may truly be the partnership your soul is seeking. A partnership of service to the divine. This does not mean you sacrifice your health or your time with precious friends. There has to be "me" time as well. It is far more important to be loved and cherished for who you are and your service to the world than what your ego has accomplished. Make sure though that you are not using career choices as escapes and avoidance of developing a closer relationship of courting love into your heart and soul even for your own personal growth and fulfillment.

I decided to do a mini survey of single people of various ages. I asked them what they loved about being single and what they did not love about being single. The ages of the group were 40's, 50's, 60's and 70's. Here are the results.

- Seventy percent of the group were female.

- The women all loved the freedom and the quiet. Every single woman who answered this survey used the word "freedom".

- All of them had been married before were divorced widowed or had been in significant relationships.

- What the women did not like was lack of connection companionship or intimacy.

Even though the age range was four generations apart the responses were the about the same.

Not one of the women said anything about missing sex. I found it interesting that the word 'freedom' was used by every female and not by any male.

Do women feel bound to a relationship where their individual self and soul do not feel free? What do you think about that question of freedom in your life? It might be interesting to review as a unique soul your sense of being free. How are your beliefs keeping you stuck or not feeling free with or without a partner?

Thirty percent of the group were men. Oddly enough the men did not mention sex either which was refreshing. The men were in their 40's and 50's and were all single. Some had been married and all had been in significant relationships in the past. The interesting comments from the men were that while single, they enjoyed the variety of choices.

- What the men did not love about being single was also the lack of companionship; the same as women.

- They also missed intimacy and deep intellectual connection.

- One of the things they did not miss was dealing with the insecurities of a partner.

I often wonder if men and women realize how similar their desires in returning to the lost art of loving is. In fact the desires for love are very similar.

There are times I miss my single life however in the marriage I have now I have very few limitations and actually am happily marred. When I met Floyd on our first date I said,

"Look, you need to know that my relationship with the Universe will always come first.

It's not a cop out; it's who I am." I have tremendous freedom of choices. Take a look at your life. Are you dating your job? I am talking to men and women here. What can you dial down? What can you save for another day? The world will not fall apart if you are not glued to your laptop 24/7. Put the electronics away and go play. Your mind and soul will love you for this gift of time that you can never recapture again.

Embrace and love your single life; not the life someone says you should have. Being alone does not mean you need to be lonely. You have the entire Universe by your side.

Try not to isolate yourself. Don't be afraid to ask friends for help if you need it. I lived the Superwoman Syndrome for many years and it wasn't fun; it was exhausting. You cannot do it all yourself. You can only be truly free when your soul rests peacefully on the pillow of your heart.

I would like to address this issue to all the advertising companies out there and tell them to knock it off. You are setting up a belief that for many is just not true. Happiness has nothing to do with being single or married. That label should never define us. It is the freedom and joy we bring to our lives no matter what our standard of living is.

Being married is not the goal or end game for many people. There is a large segment of the population that is so fed up with this advertising tirade. We are very tired of your message that something is wrong because a person is not attached to someone else. You are selling fear; not love.

If you are content with being single and have no desire to have a partner then lets go over a few guidelines for inner contentment.

- Stop comparing yourself to anyone else who is in a relationship that appears perfect. There is no such thing as a perfect relationship.

- Accept that being single has amazing benefits and can be a blessing not a curse.

- Love who you are and how you live your life.

- Happiness is a quality of the soul being at peace. It is a direct result of your relationship with your own spirit mind feelings and how you live your life on this temporary place known as Earth.

I apologize for repeating this time and time again but it really is important to know thyself. It is an age old saying that was inscribed on the entrance to ancient temples.

Know thyself and discover love. Know thyself and know love and divine wholeness.

Know thyself and merge with your soul. Know thyself and be the master of your mind and the mistress of your heart and soul. You don't have to go to therapy forever. Stop over analyzing everything in your mind. You will probably make yourself crazy with the whys and why nots that took you off your path of agape and being whole, or so you thought. You need only to have the desire to remember what happiness and joy feel like.

If you are single and have the spiritual desire to date remember that dating should be considered a source of practice with applied discernment. Approach it with an attitude of fun and discovery, not waiting for a disaster. Not everyone you meet is going to lead into an intimate partnership and there is real value in just having friends with the other sex. If you are a single serial dater, you may want to consider just meeting people for friendship to do things with and nothing more. It is a good start and a good adjustment from dating every person who walks in front of you thinking that he or she is that illusive "one". I formed many male friendships and was fine with spending time hanging out with men just as tennis pals and nothing more. It was easy and there was no pressure. Many men opened up to me about their own lives and relationships and I really learned a lot about men. The friendships were wonderful. I was a single woman who cherished her life, all her friends both male and female and felt no pressure to prove myself to anyone.

I met a widower once a really great guy named Ron. We both played tennis and enjoyed each other's company. He had not been single very long. Whenever he talked about his deceased wife he would sob his heart out. It was so sad to see this. I asked him if he wanted to talk about it and he said he couldn't. He told me that every time he thought about her he couldn't stop crying. I asked if he had done any grief counseling and he told me that he had not. He then told me his daughter had made him promise not to bring any woman into her mother's house ever. She further told him she would not accept any "other" woman moving one of his wife's belongings. I asked him if all her personal items were still in the house and they were. The thought of his daughter doing this made him cry even more. This poor man was lost. He wasn't ready to build a relationship with anyone but himself.

I really liked Ron, and I felt he was no where near even dating a woman just for company because he felt guilty dating. He asked me what he should do. I told him that I loved spending time with him but that I didn't think he was really ready to date. I felt he was still grieving the death of his wife. I suggested that he take some time for himself and get things sorted out. I told him that I would still love to play tennis and remain friends with him if he was okay with that. He wasn't and was insulted that I was only offering casual friendship.

Here is a salient point as a single person who is dating. This applies to men and women.

If you want to build a true partnership with the foundation of friendship first you have to remember first of all to be honest. You don't expose your entire life on the first few dates; you are interviewing for a compatibility connection. If someone needs professional help, it's not your place to suggest that. It is not your job to be the other person's daily therapist their mother or father career counselor or the go to person for entertainment purposes. It can potentially drain you and you won't be filled with sharing love. You are sharing your opinions of life based on your own experiences. The end result of this story is that a few years later Ron and I did connect on a social media site. He was no longer single. He had gotten married to a wonderful woman. He had moved from his former home. He was very happy and I was happy for him.

Cosmic Karmic Relationships

Karma has gotten a bad rap. It is not good or bad. Karma is merely unfinished business.

Karma or unfinished business will follow you through lifetimes until you fulfill the karmic contract and transcend it. You are free of that karmic debt of unfinished business for the journey of your soul. You may have brought it forward from lifetimes ago or you may have created it in this lifetime. This unfinished business is still something you need to learn so the lesson repeats. Once the lesson becomes knowledge and you put your get smart hat on you no longer need to repeat those lessons. Finally, what a relief.

The best example I can give of karma is a black ink spot on a white piece of fabric.

There it is waiting to be cleansed and cleared away. When you transcend the karma, the lesson is no longer needed and the black ink spot disappears as it is negated. Part of your karma can also be a return to a soul group from the past. This can be family friends or individual people you had a deep harmonious relationship with. You may simply have a desire to continue that relationship in another lifetime. Life is often considered the karmic classroom of the Universe with various levels of evolution or education.

My husband told me after dating others for awhile that when I walked up to him on our first date, he said to himself, "Ah there you are!" When I asked him what he meant about that, he said he felt that he knew me even though we had never met in this lifetime. He believed it was from another lifetime. He was also very familiar to me. I was pretty comfortable with him even from the first date. We definitely had an instant connection.

About a month after we were dating, I had a past life dream. I felt I was watching a familiar story unfold from the past. What I saw in the dream was that I was standing on a curved rugged stone stairway on the side of a house. It was hot dry and dusty. I was in a desert environment and saw palm trees. I was watching a man get on a horse who was my husband at the time. I recognized him as the man I was currently dating. We had five children who were running around a group of horses. He was a soldier and had on a certain type of uniform with a flowing cape. He was holding some kind of head gear in his hand. This was a very ancient time that I felt was either in Greece or Rome.

"Don't worry Ill be back," he said. I remember grasping the stairway wall my right hand knowing I would never see him again in that lifetime. I floated to a later period in the dream to a room where I saw myself crying. He had been killed.

I told him about the dream on a date one night and he nodded his head. He said, "Well I guess I finally did get back to you. It just took a few lifetimes." I felt he was keeping his promise that he would come back. Oddly enough, in this lifetime he is a retired helicopter pilot for a police department so I guess he decided to be a soldier in some form once again. It is very possible you may meet someone in this lifetime that immediately is very familiar to you. Your souls recognize each other. What you agreed to do in the world of spirit was to return to each other at some in time and complete your karmic contract or create a new one.

A karmic contract has two sides to the unfinished business. Each soul has agreed to complete the karma for themselves not the other person. This is important because often people ask me whether their karma contract is done with a certain person or must they stick around until it is complete. The answer is no. I think many people stay in relationships because the other person is not done with their lessons which is not necessary.

If you are done with the relationship and have had your ah ha moments of growth as a person and evolution of the soul, you don't need to stick around, waiting for the other person to complete their half of the contract. If you are joyfully staying in a relationship while the other person is working on their karmic issues and you see the value in creating a brand new relationship then hang in there and negotiate a new relationship. The main issue is to always remember never to judge the journey of another. Through the life lessons and the law of cause and effect for every action there is a reaction. Through right effort you will receive great benefits in your karma for now and in the future individually and as a couple.

The karmic lessons of life are hard to take sometimes. It would be wise to look deeper at what needs to change if you feel you hit the repeat button on your life often. There is a big difference between being smart and being wise. Having knowledge or being smart comes from learning karmic lessons through the University of Life. You grow as a person. Yet the soul stands there saying, "Hey what about me? You told me you would take those lessons and never repeat them again. I saw you doing the same thing over and over again in making those choices. You are riding around on the lawnmower of life and nothing is getting mowed down. You cannot expect a different result if the weeds keep popping up again and again. You know that definition of insanity right? It makes the soul weep."

The soul is the compilation of all you have ever been in the past are now in the present moment and all you shall be in future lifetimes. Imagine that inside of you is this amazing light called your divine spark or spirit. This spirit is the spark of life that is on assignment for this one lifetime you are living right now. When you are born, this active energy or spark of life that is illuminated connects you to the soul's memory. This everything you learned from each lifetime. Think of the soul as a warehouse that stores all of those lifetimes. Each lifetime has a unique spirit, which is born and becomes you.

When you die the spirit lifts out of the body and returns to its full form in the Universe, your soul's warehouse.

The spirit for each lifetime has an identity which determines how where and with whom you will experience or live your life. It is part of a predetermined destiny that is written in the divine plan which is co-authored by you and the Universe along with your spiritual guides and teachers. These guides and teachers exist in the hologram of the Universe and their purpose is to assist you in having the best life experience possible. When you pray meditate or are out in nature you may feel a presence. This feeling you have connects you to the memory of the many journeys of the soul. This is why some people are inspired in this state because the soul remembers everything.

Many people have memories or flash backs of previous lives. They may even have done past life regression. The purpose of remembering a past is not to remind you that you karmically were once the Queen of Egypt or Cleopatra. The positive purpose is to determine what you brought forth into this lifetime to continue to improve on or karmically correct. A karmic correction is to balance out the old business that didn't get finished. It can often include people with whom you had relationships in the past. This can be your parents siblings friends lovers or marriage partner, etc. This is often why when you meet someone, although you really do not know them, you feel like you do because this is soul recognition. It feels familiar. Often people consider this person to be a soul mate.

You have the ability if you are awake and aware to experience something from a past life that you may need to pay attention to. Haven't you had the experience of running into someone again and again? Do you ever wonder why? Is this a plain coincidence or is your spirit trying to give you a gently boot in the butt to pay attention. Personally, I don't think there are any coincidences. You may want to pay attention or if you wish you can also ignore it. You do have freewill. Your spirit and the Universe, of which you are a part not independent of, are very invested in your evolution. The spirit wakes up soul memory and sometimes it is pushed away. Then it keeps pushing because the soul has a desire to serve you as a person growing on the Earth through lessons and knowledge gained. Once again, when you apply that knowledge and do life differently, you are accessing the eternal wisdom of the soul which is part of the entire Universe.

The soul is the entirety of your experience and is passionately desiring that you do something different to change your life so you can be happier and whole. I have heard from my clients frequently that the same type of person keeps coming into their lives who will not commit. They are not honorable nor do they respect them. Again and again this type of person keeps showing up. They know and recognize the character flaws of this person. The Universe says, "Okay one more time." How many times must this type of person show up until you say, "No thanks, been there, done that, no need for more." Right then and there you took the knowledge you learned from your experience and applied it. You applied it because you do not repeat a lesson that tears you apart and brings you to your knees screaming at God. You do life differently and now the soul sighs and says, "Wow, they finally got it. No need to give them that experience ever again."

The lesson has been learned and applied. The choices now come from wisdom instead of repeating the same dance over and over again. You elevate from the classroom of negative chaos into the karmic classroom of choice. You have graduated from the school of playing life into the University of Wisdom. It is your divine inheritance from the Universe that allows your spirit to soar. Suffering does not belong to a soul that is equal balanced wise and free. That freedom comes from spiritual wisdom.

Even in the realm of spirit when you are not in bodily form you are gaining wisdom. The karma you now create sits on your heart like your Universal badge of accomplishment.

This creates a lineage of wisdom to live out in all lifetimes ahead of you. This action of doing life differently and using wisdom in your choices removes the same drama of disappointment and sets you karmically free.

This new field of awareness and wisdom feeds the etheric body or soul emanation. This magnetic field of resonance expands the magnetics of the Over-Soul. Then the Law of Attraction is activated. This Law of Attraction is your field of soul emanation vibrating and drawing people, experiences and opportunities to you yet again continuing the dance of soul expansion. This is created by a consciousness shift when you perceive your life as changed. You are actually doing things differently as well. This is not specific to personal relationships but with all relationships. The world becomes a new playground.

You can actually feel something shift inside of you. Voila the people who show up appear to be different. Are they different or is it because you are? You are the one who is different and as a result gifted yourself the blessings of applying wisdom. People appear to be kinder attentive respectful and more loving. It started with you. In the Law of Attraction like attracts like. How amazing life becomes when you love yourself enough to change within and without.

At this point you may decide what I thought I had decided which was to embrace my life without any yearning for a partner. You may find the quality of your friends to be deeper. New people arrive in friendship and you are shedding and releasing those old friends who you are now learning really weren't friends at all. When you change, your world changes. This may be such a revelation to you. You don't need or want someone to date or create a life with.

Give yourself a break and some time to love that person you have become. Have a love affair with you. The great Buddha teaches that what you create in this lifetime you will take to the next. Use this lifetime to clean your cup of karma and fill it with overflowing love. Look at what you carry with you into your futures waiting behind the veils of time.

The Law of Equals and Opposites

I know you have all heard the saying that opposites attract. Part of that is true from a spiritual perspective. There is negative energy and positive energy and they are equal.

Each has a purpose as a form of energy to move you forward in life. The terms negative and positive are referring to the mechanics or the vibration of energy. Like the battery in your car you need both poles of energy to make that battery spark so the engine comes to life. You can't move too well with a dead battery in your car. If we look at a car as a symbol of your life, i.e., something that moves you and your soul forward, it won't go anywhere without these positive and negative charges. These are aspects of your own soul and the soul of other people projected onto each other through experience. This is often referred to as the polarities of life or the dualistic nature of the soul.

Through the Law of Equals you can only love another to the level you love yourself.

What does that really mean for you personally? How do you love yourself? How do you know love as a state of being content and happy? Is love a constant companion that is always with you or an idea of long ago? There is no prince on a white horse that will come and save you. You will not give a woman your sword to hold while you are off to the holy wars waiting and pining for your return. In the Aquarian Age courtship begins with you and is shared with another. In order to accomplish this successfully you first have to court and save yourself. Then call in love and welcome to be shared if this is your desire. Perhaps we have replaced the word courtship with the word romance. What do courtship and romance have in common if anything at all?

Define for yourself what courtship means and how you wish to be courted. Get clear on what a relationship really means to you and be honest with your answers. We court jobs family and friends. We court lovers. We court the heavens each time we pray. If you don't open the door of your heart to equal and loving relationships you are missing out on a huge opportunity to share the lost art of loving. Grab a pencil and a piece of paper and start to write down the words courtship and relationships. What would that look like in your life?

The Law of Equals reminds you that as a soul each person that crosses your path is equal to your soul. They are the same. Through the Law of Equals you are seeing through the reflection of that person your own energy bouncing back at you. If you are activating the 181

Law of Equals, the person drawn to you is there to be of service to your soul and to their own soul as well. The same applies for you with them. The Law of Equals is related to the fact that all souls are created with the same glue of the Universe which is love. We are all created equally as a being of love. Always. Each soul is as unique as a crystal of snow and beautiful in its own special way. If you love purely and equally from the vibration of the soul connecting, you align from the ideal nature of the soul. When you align with the ideal nature of the soul you have tapped into divine wisdom of the higher mind of superconsciousness. Wisdom is your ability to remember the call of the soul at all times to feel and remember one thing. The presence of love.

The Law of Opposites on the planet reveals the extremes of duality. We live in a world of polar opposites. We even have a north and south pole on the earth to balance each other. If we are awake and aware of the higher power of our own spirit, we have the ability to connect to the Universal planes of awareness to find our own inner balance.

We have the extremes of peace and war representing love and fear. The place of inner balance is a palace of harmony that moves us beyond the extremes into a greater state of soul consciousness. It is your center. Although there are wars on the earth, we have faith and hope that a better way can be achieved. We do have experiences of people who are behaviorally negative and positive which can spark a negative or positive emotional response. It is more than love them or leave them. We can reject them or embrace them.

Often when we first meet a person, we are attracted by all the things we have in common.

We feel we are equal. They like the same food and the same music. They even get the same coffee drink we do at Starbucks. This has got to be a match made in heaven. We are so similar, so equal!

We are naturally drawn to someone, even a friend, who we believe is similar. It validates us at some subconscious level. We advance from the lower or limited realms of life on the earth as a person and connect into the higher divine realms of the high holy heart.

When we advance from limitations and judgment and make this alignment, we honor the Law of Equals. You actually vibrate or exist in a higher state where everything is equal.

There is no separation. There is only wholeness. This strengthens our soul and feeds us just like the battery charge that is needed to keep the car moving forward. We develop spiritual strength because the soul's nature is the ideal nature. What we attract and call in through the Law of Equals is an opportunity person or experience that gives us the ability to attain that spiritual strength to move us forward. The continual journey lifts up your life again and again to a place of continual growth and evolution of the ascended soul.

Conflict exists in a relationship when we bounce back and forth mentally and emotionally. Remember that it starts with your thoughts and feelings first. You are responsible for that. No one makes you think or feel anything. It is such a struggle when we sometimes bounce back and forth. One day we see the negative and the next day we see the positive. The game changer for reaching a feeling of happiness and being whole is your ability to learn from both the dark and the light. The negative and positive are teachers for greater wisdom. You can only watch one movie of life at a time and the first one is yours. This type of review from a point of clarity not judgement allows you to see what you need to learn about yourself.

Blame begins to melt away like a soft gentle bead of water falling on the leaf of a flower.

"It's their fault" no longer applies. Taking ownership of your behavior is the sign of an evolved soul. Do you always see what is wrong with someone or what is right with someone? Fear is part of our lower nature. It separates us from love. If you have the desire to live from your soul, your choices are love bound. In the Law of Equals and the Law of Opposites we are all connected to a Universe that is harmonious. Try not to be your own personal prophet of doom and gloom predicting failure for your future. The soul will feed you if you allow it to. Live today and nourish your soul well.

How to Spiritualize All Relationships

Here you are a newly reborn person with an amazing happy outlook on life. You have gathered a pearl. You feel wise in your choices both professional and personally. You are content. You sleep better than you ever have ever before. You feel lucky. Life is showing up instead of shutting down. You review your old friendships. Some you keep and others you feel it may be time to release. Life should never be about all or nothing.

Your spirit has gifted you with freewill and discernment. No one's opinion of you is more important than your own. This is how you honor your soul. You serve your soul.

You are not being selfish. You are not better. You know you are wiser. You feel you really have learned how to spiritualize relationships.

Just when you think everything is almost perfect those life lessons show up again. They challenge you to grow just a little bit more and push your soul to even greater evolution.

Then what do you do with people around you who are constantly negative? Do you completely dump them from your life? What if you work with someone like this every day? What if you are in a relationship with someone like this? What if a family member is like this?

How can we spiritualize relationships with negative people? I often think that life is a cosmic joke because just when you have reached a place of inner peace, wham, you get whacked with a new reality that life is not perfect. Through the Law of Reflection we get to see this acted out by the people around us. We also get to see how we emotionally react to all people negative and positive in the dance of duality. The people whose life's goal is to share all their sorrows and suffering with you each and every time you are with them is very draining. Here you are on the mountaintop of the Universe with all your divine wisdom and now you slipped down the hill into everyday life. The culprit is the person who loves to tell you everything that is wrong with their life rather than what is right with their life? This is a biggie.

Everyone knows someone who has a story to tell. You are on a merry-go-round that never stops and get really tired on this negativity ride. This is negative behavior not negative energy. Remember you cannot grow if you are not happy. You cannot evolve unless you are wise. It is not your job to teach anyone other than yourself unless someone asks for your wisdom. However, how do you survive the drain of someone dumping their negative stuff on you time after time without running out of the room as if your hair is on fire? These are probably your brain cells in the nervous system about to blow.

The first way to handle this negativity is to stop and review how you played the game of the Law of Equals with this person. How did you create or give permission to hearing all of this negative stuff? Did you sit and complain all the time over and over again wishing life could be different? Did you feed each other's negativity? How to stop the merry-go-round is simply this; stop feeding your own negative behavior. It is a vibration and everyone can feel it. Have you ever walked into a room and felt like you could cut the air with a knife? It is heavy energy. Even if you cannot see it, you can definitely feel it. If you want to continue with your downer of a story of everything in life that went wrong, keep it up because you reap what you sow. If negative people are always coming to you complaining, do they want advice wisdom or merely a dumping ground for their own pain?

You may have a great opportunity to help someone move out of negativity unless they are so invested in staying in the mud no one can move them. It is their karma drama not yours. We are told to live in the present moment and let the future take care of itself. In that present moment, the heart and soul do their greatest work of evolution. If a person is talking constantly about their past, they are reliving it and taking you on the journey with them which is backwards. Consider using this one sentence with a person who is negative all the time, "I hear what you are saying about your past. How does that affect what you have learned about yourself where you are today? How do you go forward?"

You may need to repeat that a number of times. It is a gentle nudge not an angry fed up shove.

Although you may want to help someone, be kind and only give advice when it is asked of you. This is called the Law of Non-Interference. It is one of the first spiritual teachings I was given when training as a professional psychic. You never give advice unless you have been given permission to deliver it. If you interfere, you have now interfered in this person's karmic life path. Now part of their karma becomes yours. I believe you have enough of your own.

A former acquaintance of mine decided later in life to try dating again. She is very attractive and intelligent. She was disappointed over and over again with the dates she went on. She never had a second date. She told me about one of her dates which was shocking to me. She said she knew immediately that she did not want to date this guy she had just met ten minutes previously. She didn't give him any time to tell her about herself or discover anything about him. Apparently he was not up to her standards although I often wonder how you can learn this in ten minutes. In any event, she stayed for a little bit and finished her glass of wine. She did at least give him that. At the end of the date she leaned over and said to him, "Now I want to tell you everything you did wrong on this date because it will help you for the next time. I have no interest in you but perhaps if you do this differently on the next date with someone else, you will have a better chance." Oh my god, why don't you just castrate the guy in front of the entire restaurant! I was beyond shocked because this woman had studied spiritual teachings for a long time.

My point here is exactly this. Do not interfere and let your ego lead the way. Do it with love and kindness because this is a person's heart and soul you are dealing with. Do not be a spiritual hypocrite. Like attracts like in the Universe. Be kind to the people who cross your path. If you want kindness you have to be kind first. Maybe this sounds like a simple thing to you. There is so much anger on the planet right now. You have to move beyond it into your own heart instead of being heartless. This is an extreme example of a negative person and interfering in someones karma. My only hope is that this man found a wonderful woman to tell him everything that is right with him instead of what is wrong.

You can heal many hearts without saying a word. The art of loving is filled with the sound of caring kind words that can heal a wounded heart. Spiritualizing a relationship is wrapped in all the aspects of the higher dimensions of the Universe. You spiritualize a relationship with understanding compassion awareness, and kindness. Have we as a race of people forgotten to be kind? Have we forgotten to be good? Have we forgotten to simply smile at a complete stranger? Did we leave our moral compass in the trash can?

Do we put someone else before our own immediate needs?

Our soul is a storage vessel of memory. Sometimes that memory gets overridden by our emotions of the moment. We get very trapped into thinking that what we feel is all there instead of tapping into what our eternal self truly knows. The soul seeks to revisit the journey of life to reincarnate, review life through experiences and refine the journey by doing it differently. A renewal occurs within the soul when we return to the lost art of loving. We are reborn. If you are firmly committed to this rebirth, just one single thought can overcome anything. Your progressive journey to partnership that begins with you is the beginning of living a blessed life. Do not get trapped into that past. What counts is who you are now.

The Divine Romance

he divine romance is your ability to share your whole soul self with another. This is often what unknowingly attracts two souls in the first place. The libido on the other hand seems to have a mind of its own. If you wait to share making love instead of sex for the sake of sex, you allow the evolution of shared love to bring you closer. When you have learned to court your own soul you have an opportunity to uncover some magical aspects of yourself and that other person.

I feel that many people believe that chemistry is the key to happiness. Soul chemistry that is birthed out of spiritual friendship is the key to happiness. It far outweighs and outlasts sexual chemistry. It is once again a reference to the state of being whole or love.

The lost art of loving reminds us of a time in our soul's history of this connection of soul chemistry. Soul chemistry is alchemical joy. It is the natural state of the soul birthing a continuum of bliss. The characteristics of bliss that we get to enjoy are happiness, joy, and peace. It is the home of the heart, the center of the Universe, and part of why we reincarnated in the first place.

Romance that has divine intention behind it creates a greater sense of feeling secure and safe. Why is this important? When you are more secure in loving another as much as you value and love yourself, your soul is safely bound. This often can feel like a tug of war with what you know is right for you and what your body wants. Is it the needs of your body, the wants of your mind or the desire of your soul? Before you jump too soon with your libido leading the way, review what your true intention really is. Define what romance means to you beyond the material world.

There is a big difference between romantic love and divine love. There are romantic gestures that inspire deeper love. Are these romantic gestures authentic and divinely guided? The divine romance begins with your desire to connect with your soul. The spiritual nature of your soul is to share love consciously. How do you have a divine romance in your life right now and I don't mean with another person?

The material world of courtship can be a challenge. We can get attached to the outer image. If it is not soul generated the image can get foggy. It can create doubt. It can also be an amazing journey of divine reflection of each others souls. Here are some pearls to remember.

- A fully engaged soul to the divine feels connected to love and wholeness.

- The enraged soul is connected to fear and separation from all that is loving.

Romance means many things to many people and it should not be defined by things.

Loving in the new age is not always a smooth ride to joy. It has challenges and opportunities for excellence. When you court and romance the desires of the soul, you are redefining how you will romance any relationship. You will feel cherished.

If you consider romance to be an action, how about reconsidering that romance is also a state of emulating love to another? Romantic times are often the most simple of times; taking a walk talking or reading together. You cannot command and demand romance.

It has to originate from a genuine place. If someone asks you how you like to loved, tell them. This goes for both men and women. Men like to be appreciated for any little thing they do. Women like attention and to be acknowledged. Both men and women want to be respected. Don't be afraid in romancing a relationship to share what makes you happy.

Good information is priceless.

I have a male client in his forties who is such a sweetheart. He told me the other day that he is a chick magnet which is probably true due to his Facebook pages. He also told me he can get sex whenever he wants and has lots of friends with benefits. I asked him,

"How is that working out for you?" He responded "Well, it's okay but it's not what I want. I really am lonely. I would love a true romantic partner."

He told me he really wants a partner he can build a life with. He is bored with the game.

It just doesn't fill him up. We talked about that longing for more. For starters, we agreed that the urge to merge immediately sexually is just too easy. He told me that the women make it too easy for the men. Wowsers! One part of him liked this and the other part of him just wanted that one special woman. It was interesting listening to him. He told me that many women are so open minded about sex that this is all a playground for passion and nothing more.

He said, "Listen, it's crazy out there. Anything goes, lots of experimenting going on. I can't figure this women thing out. They just meet you and having sex is expected." Here is a man saying that women are too promiscuous.

This man is in the prime of his life and is tired of playing the game. He wants divine romance pure and simple. I am happy to report while writing this that he stopped all the crazy dating as he called it. He spent time alone. He got clear. He now is in love with a wonderful woman with two sons who adore him. He tells me all the time, "I am so happy.

I trusted myself and my soul. I asked for divine help and look who I got."

There is a great celebration in the Universe when two souls consciously come together to share divine romance. It is worth the wait if this is what you desire. You deserve to be cherished by another but only if you cherish yourself first. I know you live in an age of technology when anything is possible at anytime. Instant gratification. Then you race off to something or someone else. Teenage years are the years of experimentation and stretching the boundaries. You want your independence. Work with your parents in boundaries that work for both of you. Dating in groups is honorable and can be a lot of fun. Stop racing through life, keep pace with your soul and know when to slow down. Sex is a function. Divine romance is profound when the time is right between two evolved and mature souls. I urge you to treasure the pearls of wisdom within.

The Divine Marriage of Soul and Self

I have met many people who are married for a long time and some who are newly married. Some are young and some are not so young. When we went to Maui to get married in a Hawaiian wedding ceremony on a beach we decided to go to a large luau as part of our honeymoon. The venue was very large so they had tables for eight people.

They sat us with other honeymoon couples and of course we could have been their grandparents. Everyone was in a great mood to celebrate their marriages. The stories started to roll around the table from each couple on how they had met. It was fun to listen and observe.

Two of the couples were in their twenties and one was in their late thirties. There was a Hindu couple at our table, and the bride was still covered with her wedding henna on her hands. Her husband was very jovial, and she was sweet and shy. They were silly together and seemed very happy. I asked them about their ceremonies because I knew enough about Hindu marriages to know the party went on for days. They had 800 people at their wedding. The husband explained that in his culture many of these people they did not even know. He then said to me, "I got some advice from my uncles though on how to be happy in my marriage." I asked him if he had heard the saying 'happy wife, happy life'.

He laughed and told me his uncles instructed him to always be attentive to his wife and never neglect her or take her for granted. He gave me a huge smile and his new bride a hug.

I decided to ask the other two men at the table how they felt about 'happy wife happy life'. One couple was a second marriage and the husband said he was going to do it differently this time. He had learned from his past mistakes. His new wife told me that she felt she had a wonderful husband. They loved doing similar things with their collective children. She also told me how important it was for her to have a husband who was also a partner and a friend. She explained that in merging two households there were a lot of challenges but as a team they managed to make everything work.

The third young man was very quiet. His very pretty wife kept giving me these odd looks and finally said in a loud voice, "Why did you get married anyway at your age?" 'Okay now I really do feel old', I thought. I told her that we got married for companionship and partnership. My husband jumped in and said loudly we married for love. Bless his heart.

Thank God he did not say we got married for hot sex, or I would have shot him.

She seemed confused as to why a senior couple would even need to be married. I asked her husband how married life was going so far. "Here is what I don't get. Sometimes I have to say I am sorry, and I don't even know what I am saying I am sorry for. I just sit there and say it because she tells me to. I had to move from my home in

Chicago to her home in Texas which I hate. I did it because I love her. I just wish I could figure out what I am saying I am sorry for all the time." I felt so sorry for this young man and I hope their marriage works out.

The Hindu man said that his uncles told him he was to say he was sorry and ask for forgiveness if he did something wrong. "It is my job to protect her heart." I was thrilled to hear that the advice from his elder family members was important to him. He seemed to respect their wisdom and advice. Once again, his quiet wife smiled her sweet smile which lit up her entire face.

The couple who had married for the second time had learned from the past. That was fairly obvious. What I loved most was their discussion about being a team. If your partner is your best friend and your teammate, you have a good winning combination.

The divine marriage has to start with your marriage to your own soul then to the Universe and then the commitment to the life of another. If you start your marriage by building on the foundation of spiritual friendship, you are laying a solid foundation of building a profound partnership.

In the marriage ceremonies around the world, as complex as an 800 guest Hindu wedding ceremony that lasts for days or a simple hand holding ceremony of the Southwest, you are standing before the entire Universe making a commitment. You are creating together a bonded karmic contract of unity that is the celebration of the joining of two souls.

It is probably one of the most sacred covenants there is to join your soul to another in marriage.

It should not be taken lightly. The family of humanity often throws marriages away like used Kleenex. It is useful for awhile and then thrown out. Divorce that is too easy to be had is often an excuse for not working on partnership issues. You will take those issues into another relationship if you don't work on yourself first. The race to the altar is not a race to happiness. Define for yourself what you feel a true partner and teammate is before you get married, not after. If you need support from your partner, tell them. If you need emotional support, please be specific.

The divine marriage is a marriage of respect, honor, commitment, dedication and devotion. The divine purpose of marriage is the divine purpose of life. How wonderful that your beloved is as devoted as you are to continuing to make your love grow. You are still each an individual with your own light, your own soul and your own life. That does not get swallowed up by a marriage. You do not suffer for love, you serve love.

There have got to be times in a marriage or any valued relationship that the needs of your partner come before the needs of yourself. This is how we serve love as a state of being that exists in each other. We honor the divine in each other. This has to be done joyfully with an open mind and heart.

There will be times you may be disappointed. If you let that disappointment fester, it can turn to resentment which can lead to anger. Anger is birthed from fear and separates you from love. Please do not let any resentment fester without trying to heal what is hurting you. Before you even get married talk about how you both would like to handle any challenges that come up. What is the best way for me to approach you with a problem?

How can we be partners and teammates with any outside obstacles that show up? How can I help you when times are tough even if I don't understand? Keep those lines of communication open and remember, no one has to agree with everything you are saying all the time.

For the men reading this, women don't need you to figure out everything but they would love it if you just listened. Women, if you present a problem to your partner, if you want them to help you, ask and be specific. Get rid of the blame game. Work together as a team for the same goal to bring more joy and happiness to each other as a divinely bonded couple. If you can't figure things out for yourself, get some advice from a wise person you respect. Don't compare your marriage to anyone else's. More than anything else find time to play and have fun. I am a huge fan of date night, game night and 'me' days. All of them are important. Celebrate your love and always remember why you fell in love in the first place. This is your life partner, your beloved and you are blessed to discover the joy of loving with them.

You are your own personal prophet on the future success of your relationships. Don't over analyze the past or spend too much time dreaming about the future. The soul of each of you will nourish the relationship. Many people today are starving emotionally. You don't need to be one of them. Your heart and your soul is the well of fulfillment that you dip into when times are daunting. The treasure chest of love must be opened within first so you can share the joy of divine love with the people you love. Love for the sake of loving. Ask for help when you need it. Speak the song of your own soul.

We are all connected through and to a Universe that is harmonious. The growth and evolution of your marriage or committed relationship can move though faith and hope to chart a course for a better way. Like the seasons on the earth, the rhythm of the Universe moves us through change gracefully from one year to the other. Believe what you have is good, have hope that it can grow and become better each and every day.

Language of the Awakened Soul

started writing a spiritual dictionary and journal a long time ago and encourage my clients to do the same thing. Words, sounds and images can mean something entirely different for each person. I don't always trust good old Webster's on or off the Internet to give meaning to all the words and symbols out there floating around. Words as you know have power. Words hold emotion. Words tell a story and express your feelings. In this age of advanced technology, our brains are on overload. We all process information differently and as a result of how we communicate we can often be misunderstood, which is frustrating.

We had limited communication skills at one time in man's evolution. I suppose when the caveman wanted to have his meal cooked, he grunted and pointed to the fire. Pretty simple right? Did we first begin to communicate through simple gestures? As we developed as a species, so did our ability to communicate. The cave dwellers who drew on the walls with their stick figures were telling us something. The shards of pottery left behind and discovered through archeology also tell us a story. There is a theory that the sounds of the first languages came from the songs of natures. This developed into song and chanting which is a beautiful thought as it carries the heart to a higher state of being.

The scholars of the scientific study of language once again do not agree when we began to develop some style of formal verbal language or communication skills.

There is of course the traditional story in the book of Genesis which says that there was only one language where God communicated to Adam and Eve. Some attribute the confusion or creation of various languages to the story of the construction of the Tower of Babel and refer this back to the teachings of the book of Genesis. The story goes that the Tower of Babel was created so man could reach heaven. Then God looked down and saw this and said, "Are you kidding me? I want it quiet here. I am not ready for all of you to join me. I am going to confuse you by casting you out with your own unique language." That is how the story is told in some scholastic circles although I have put my own spin on it. Was there, however, a silent language that we had before the primal need to get our needs met? Were we plopped down on the earth and told, "Go figure it out smarty pants. The Universe is no longer available. We are on a permanent vacation"?

Energy has always existed. Energy has movement velocity texture and guess what else?

Energy holds sound. We were able to communicate to the Universe long before we fell from grace and the Tower of Babel was created. Have you ever heard a bird sing, sat by a rushing stream of water and not been affected? Has the wind ever spoken to you? If you really pay attention to the sounds of nature, is there a message? Nature is the canvas of the Universe. Any time we pay attention to the sounds of nature we connect to the Universe. It's a good place to start your new language of the awakened soul. Through nature you reconnect to your heart and soul because nature has always existed. It will always be.

If you live in a city where the presence of nature is limited, please bring something of nature into your home. Anything small like a plant rock or a sea shell that calls to you. If you are having a bad day, go to this item, put your fingers in the dirt or hold the seashell in your hand. Breathe. The first sounds of nature were created for you to connect to your soul. This language will always be available to awaken the heavy heart into the language of the Universe. Go to nature first. Additionally, if you and a loved one have things you really need to talk about that are important for both of you, go out into nature. Forget the favorite restaurant and the glasses of wine. Forget the kitchen table. Get out of your space and go outside. Take time to connect to the energy of the earth feel the presence of the divine then start talking. Find a place you can sit undisturbed and open your heart to the heavens first.

Sedona, Arizona is a profound natural temple for the Universe and I was happy to have experienced the sacredness of the land there for almost fifteen years. It still remains a spiritual pilgrimage site for many. The experience of being surrounded by those amazing red rocks lifts up your heart to a place it has never been before. Nature has a loud voice in Sedona. I had the honor to walk the land with a native American elder from the Hopi Nation who spent some time with me. He spoke of the elders and their vision quests. He told me of their ways in speaking the silent language of spirit. We didn't say very much on our hike but we spoke volumes with our souls.

Pay attention to the sounds of nature. If you have a spiritual journal, write down what you connect with. What speaks to you? This may give you the opportunity for an incredible healing of your entire being. We are guiding our souls naturally to a place of peace even if we are not fully aware of it. Although there are many sounds in the nature kingdom, they connect us to the silence of our own soul. It is the most profound connection with the divine so I encourage you to allow your heart to be touched and moved beyond your perceived limitations.

There is a silent way beyond nature we communicate within our soul that has always existed. It is telepathic communication. Have there ever been times you have been in a social situation where you just look at a friend or someone sitting across from you and without saying anything you know what they are thinking? Then you laugh and nod your head saying "yeah, I get it". No words are necessary. You don't need to be a PhD to know when someone is happy with you or conversely unhappy with you. You can feel it.

You know yourself when you are having a bad day just by the way you feel when you get out of bed and you stub your toes on the dresser. "Uh oh, its going to a bad day I can just feel it." This silent acknowledgement is affecting your behavior. That behavior is how you silently communicate to the world who you are.

I challenge you before you get out of bed each morning to add this to your routine.

Instead of jumping out and doing your normal routine, stay quiet even for just a moment.

Close your eyes breathe and listen. Listen to the sound of your own heartbeat. Listen to the sounds in the house. Listen to your breathing and connect. Before you open your eyes, thank the Universe for the day before you. Find one thought sound picture or symbol that shows up as a positive affirmation for what that day will be. Project that image on the template of your mind and allow yourself no matter what to hold that thought. Silent communication that is telepathic to your own soul is the ability of you co-creating with the Universe. A person who is living an ascended life will always find time at least once or twice in their day to unplug from the world and plug into their heart and soul. Give the Universe one moment and the Universe will give you a lifetime of joy.

Your job is to pay attention and be receptive.

Be mindful of how you are communicating your feelings to another by your behavior.

Your actions speak volumes of what you are thinking and feeling. Your behavior tells a huge story and it generally is immediate. Some people refer to this as attitude. If you want to experience a life that is filled with love, you have to act from a place of love first.

Monitor you language. Remember once again that everything you say think feel or do is instructions to the Universe. What is the language you are speaking to your higher self?

We all know that online bullying has been a huge problem in the younger generation.

It has been so horrific that children have taken their own lives with the despair it has created. Everything you say to another is recorded as information. Depending upon the evolution of that person, how they receive that information can destroy their soul. Has someone through their silent communication told us a story we have ignored? Have we forgotten how to listen with our heart? Words can be like daggers or kisses of bliss to the heart. How can you encourage anyone who is younger around you to be honorable with their words?

In returning to the lost art of loving, hopefully you have re-defined the art of listening as well. I don't mean with your ears. I mean with your heart first. We all have a soul song.

It plays loudly in the harmonics of the Universe. It is like a carrier wave of energy we can feel. You can feel the joy in your heart when you look at a newborn baby smiling.

You can listen to their gurgling sounds and feel happy. You are connecting to the divine innocence that a new soul reflects to you. When you are with someone, even if they have been in your life for a long time, pay attention to the non-verbal communication. Open your heart like the petals of a rose, and send them love. You don't even need to be in the same place with them. You can send telepathic love and healing to anyone, anywhere at any time. It is called silent prayer.

Talk to the divine. Don't ask for anything. Try not to over think your dialogue with divinity. It comes from your heart and your soul not your mind. Be still and go within first for the guidance to live a life that is fulfilling. We often have messengers on the Earth and don't even know it. I am referring to those people who hand you your cup of latte in the morning and give you a great smile. One of the great masters told us to be a 'smile millionaire'. Do you walk around smiling for no reason? It is often contagious.

Do you walk down the halls in your office or school with a scowl on your face? Replace it with a smile. Think of something or someone that does make you smile. Reflect that to others. You may open a door to happiness in their heart just by that one smile.

Smiling is probably the most beautiful language of the awakened soul. Pay it forward all the time. We have forgotten we are all spiritual brothers and sisters. One day, smile for the sake of smiling and see how your world can begin to change. This type of joyful telepathic soul to soul language is the most powerful of all.

The language of the awakened soul is filled with goodness grace honor intention commitment and caring. Although we live in an age of self-reliance it serves us to use language that is inclusive not exclusive. If you are always speaking from a place of "I" how can you expect a spirit of cooperation when its all about you? As I have stated many times, when you live truly from the sacredness of your own heart and spirit you embrace the world not reject it. This new spiritual unity of community that is birthing itself asks for you to use language that supports that concept. We us ours are more inclusive than I me or mine.

The Divine Plan is a record book of experience. Make yours interesting and unique!

—Johanna Carroll

PART V

SEASONS OF LOVE

Preface

We live out our reincarnation as a soul moving from lifetime to lifetime. Each of these lifetimes has a season to it. A past life may have felt light and warm just like summer.

Another lifetime may have felt cold and oppressive like the winter of your soul especially if you lived in times of war or the Inquisition. This lifetime is a culmination of multiple seasons or lifetimes of living on the Earth as as a soul in a body. The journey of our soul therefore is seasonal in nature as these lifetimes weave through the veils going back and forth.

I wanted to write a little bit about these seasons of experience from the time we are children to the day we take our last Earthly breath. Each season is a thread of experience we carry and join to the next creating the pages of our destiny as we move and evolve.

Our life is a story of many chapters and verses.

We have an opportunity to fulfil our primary destiny to return to the lost art of loving on each page of our own book of life. Each season awaits us to wrap us in the arms of love.

No matter how young or old our soul knows the way to go.

The New Children of Love

No one can deny that the face of a small baby is the face of an angel. There is something so incredibly innocent about this small being that we revert to making sounds and gestures that we didn't even realize we knew. Why do we fall in love with babies? The moment we gaze on a baby's face we see all of beauty of divinity reflected back to us.

We see divine love that is pure new and untainted. We see the reflection of our own pure soul radiating like a beam of light right onto our heart. They remind us of who we really are and we gravitate to feel that plain simple joy once again. We feel and see love.

The new children of love that are born upon the earth all have a mission just like we do. In the past forty years many of these soul groups of children have been put into various categories. They are referred to as the indigo, crystal and rainbow children. Each category had a specific color attached to it. Some said they could see in the area around the head called the auric body. Within that aura, or field of energy, some also saw colors.

There have been many teachings written in the past about how these categories and colors define a child their future and their behavioral style that is or will be predominant. What many healers were beginning to see in the new generations being born was a different kind of child that was so unique that the traditional school systems and traditional beliefs in psychology had some challenges. Many parents were very invested in the kind of child they had brought into the world and what type of child they were. They also were concerned on how they could best serve that child as a teacher and spiritual guide which was and still remains admirable.

The spiritual teachings on the Earth remind us that we are the guardians of the innocent soul of a child. They are born helpless and need a guiding hand even for the simplest of tasks. Parents teach through their actions and example all the time. Even a small baby follows the sound of a parent's voice almost immediately. In any event, children do change us. They are the bearer of a new era of light and love here on the planet Earth to heal. Children are considered the spiritual flowers that grace our earth. With the nourishment of love and mindful guidance, like the garden of life for these precious spiritual flowers, we have to prepare and cultivate the soil.

The new children of love are here to remind us simply of one thing which is to be love. These amazing small souls have a huge job to do in shifting the consciousness of humanity. Although their mission may seem simple you already know that man makes things very complicated at times. The world is at a tipping point, a choice of inner love or acting in outer fear. The new children of love are here to break through the barriers that are now polarizing us globally. They are here to heal what is broken to bring us into a time of unity and harmony instead of that which is breaking us in half. We are seeing generations of very wise children being born with amazing natural talents that no one has taught them at least in this lifetime. We do as a new soul bring forth talent from another lifetime as well as certain preferences. All habits are stored in the soul as well as these natural gifts. How can a parent explain their child who is an amazing artist, musician or opera singer to the world?

Although what counts is who this child is in this lifetime, the unexplainable gifts and talents seem to be related to a significant life of accomplishment in the past. A spiritual explanation is that this child had a desire to have another lifetime and to bring the memory of those gifts through the veils of reincarnation. Many times we recognize someone in our life today who was a child in another lifetime. The big trick is what to do with that relationship today.

Over twenty years ago I received a phone call from a woman on the east coast who had been referred to me. As soon as I spoke with her, I felt a profound emotional connection.

We routinely did session work together. She came on many retreats that I offered to my clients so I had the pleasure of meeting her in person. Her energy filled the whole room no matter where she was. She immediately became one of the many spiritual daughters I have on the Earth. I had offered a spiritual retreat on a cruise ship. During one of the quiet session times we had together a past life vision popped in like it often does.

I immediately felt I was being pulled strongly to the left which for me is a sign my guides are taking me back into the past. Sometimes it is the past in this lifetime, sometimes I can actually feel like I have traveled through various doors or levels into past lives. In any event, when I am in a past life I know it. When I looked down at my feet in this vision, I saw dusty feet with no shoes on. When I lifted my head, I saw that there was a woman standing in the middle of a large circle of people. I felt I was standing in a village in the jungle because I could smell and hear the sounds of the jungle and saw primitive huts behind the circle. In the arms of the woman was a small child. The woman was very young. The medicine man of the tribe was waving a huge branch of a tree with something wrapped on the outer edge tapping on the woman. He was yelling at her.

There was a woman behind him who I knew immediately was the wife of the chief of the tribe. She was ranting and raving and was obviously really upset with this young girl. The ceremony I was watching was her being thrown out of the tribe. She had been ostracized by her tribe because the baby she had was the chief's child. She was accused by the wife of seducing the chief. The truth was that the chief of the tribe had been pursuing this young lady sexually for some time and had actually raped her in the jungle when she was alone. Even her own mother could not save her.

The next scene the young woman is walking up a large mountain alone with her baby.

She had no possessions food or shelter. She was abandoned along with her small child. In past life readings my experience is that there are flashes of pictures or scenes that scroll by me. Then they stop and I can view what is happening. It is sort of like a fast forward on your remote control that takes you to the next part of the movie you are watching. The last scene I had was one of those fast forward moments. I knew intuitively that it was a few weeks after the scene in the village. The woman was starving. She was scraping her fingers into the dirt to find roots for her child who was bloated with hunger. I felt her getting dizzy. I heard the baby crying. At that point, it was like a bolt of lightening hit me. I was the woman and the baby was

Alison in this lifetime. When I opened my eyes to look at her and report this, she was holding her throat and crying. She knew before I even said it that we both died on that mountain hungry for food and more hungry for love and acceptance. From that day forward, Alison and I became even closer because of this memory. Why did this child of mine from another lifetime return in the form of a spiritual daughter?

First of all for me, I was thrown out of the tribe as an innocent. No one protected me. I was blamed for something I never did. In this lifetime, my birth family basically threw me out of the tribe as well. I am not telling you this for you to feel sorry for me, there is a silver living in everything. As a result of the past life experience once again in this lifetime, I had a chance to reclaim the true love of my daughter Alison. I live an amazing life without the approval of any tribe. Alison now had a spiritual mom who could show her not only how to survive in the world but how to thrive which she is doing beautifully.

The point is you have an opportunity in this life time to remember the precious soul of a child from a previous life and possibly have that same child participate in your life now.

It really is amazing when you think of the soul connection possibilities. Many times we chose to be born once again as children into the same soul group or family, whether birth or extended family. I will never forget the feeling of dying in that lifetime with rocks and dirt in my mouth watching my small baby die because of jealousy. Gratefully, we found each other again and feed each others souls all the time.

Conversely, many parents cannot imagine where this child of theirs even came from because they are so different from anyone else in their family. Once again a child chooses the parents as the first hand to guide them not control them. Whether you like the teenager that feels like a hostile enemy in your home, they are there to karmically heal.

Many teens are in emotional inner battles. The hard part is often hidden from the parents.

The fiery personality of the teenager which is so contrary for some has shown up in your home to purify negative karma.

I found when my children turned teenagers I immediately became stupid. Luckily that didn't last too long. I was amazed at some of their behavior and found that as long as I remained consistent and practiced tough love, eventually the tide turned. I know that as parents we feel we are the authority figure for our children. What you say goes.

However, a safe place to talk can be initiated at any age. You expect your child to listen to everything you say but how can you start listening to your child? You don't have to agree with what they are saying but it will serve you in the future if you can listen even for five minutes without reacting.

The heart and mind of a child records everything. For those of you who have done cognitive therapy you already know about the child and parent tapes. Those are the recorded tapes of information on how a child learns to live a life by merely observing the experience. It is what they know through example and the game of life played out on the stage of their hearts. Although my ex-husband and I never argued or yelled at each other, my older son told me after our divorce that he knew we were angry. Really how did you know that? "Well, I felt it," he said, "I just knew." It registered. I never forgot that.

The new children of love being born on the earth now are very wise souls. I feel they have come to teach us all something very wise. Children will face many choices in their lives. There is so much outside stimulation that their choices, just like ours, will overwhelm them. When you put down a guideline for the new children of love in making choices, tell them why in as simple language as you can. Did your mom ever say to you, "Because I said so," without any explanation? This will not fly with these young children. Give them an explanation that comes from love even if you only say, "Because I love you, that is why." They may just nod their head and say okay, which is fine.

A parent of an obstinate child asked me once if there was any kind of spiritual teaching I could give that might help with this child who was driving her crazy. I had suggested to her that she and her child together find a place in the house and call it 'the safe place to talk'. It was important that the child participated in the location as this was a place that on some level was sacred ground. This is not a 'time out' place. A safe place to talk is where even at a very young age you inspire the child to communicate from their heart to you. It does not mean it is only a place you go to if something bad has happened. Indeed you are creating an environment that is peaceful loving kind and receptive. Even as a small child this can be the special place where you go to just sit, hug, laugh and love.

You do not bring toys to distract or games to play. It is you and your child soul to soul.

In a safe place to talk, the parent listens. That is your job. Just listen. You do not need to judge. You do not offer advice. You receive information. You do not go running to anyone else sharing sacred information because if you do you violate your child's trust.

When you are in a safe place to talk it needs to feel comfortable. Maybe it's a step on the stairs to the house or a corner of a room with no distractions. It is you and your child.

After a few months, this parent called to report that things had changed for the better with her defiant little son. Even though her day was always busy, they regularly went to their special place to share information. He was so taken with this that he began to ask to go to the safe place to talk when something wonderful had happened and was really special. Things started to calm down. He was heard. He was loved and respected. His small world became softer and more loving. This creation of a safe place to talk from a small age opened better doorways to communication where he felt as he got older he would not be judged. He would be heard. There were times when his mother asked him if he needed some help from her. She didn't offer advice, she listened. She held him and told him she loved him. Some days that was all he needed. I don't know how old he is right now but I hope when the time calls for it, no matter where he is, he will call and say, "Mom, its time for safe place to talk."

The new children of love learn quickly. They were downloaded with tons of information before they were born and may try to race through life. Your job is to slow down the pace or assimilation that even as a small child can cause overload. Try to limit the amount of TV computer and electronic game time. The brain is being programmed by this information. It almost hypnotizes the brain and disconnects it from the soul. The mind becomes distracted and attached to the messaging of the outer world and a false imprint on the soul can be created if this is not monitored correctly.

Each child has a divine plan just like you do. They signed up for life for their own personal growth and evolution of their individual soul. You can guide them to a point and then realize that at some point they will have to fly free. I asked my mother once who had three daughters "how do you know which child to love the most?" Her answer was simple and very wise. "The one who needs it the most at that time." Not all children will walk the same path. Let them sing their own song. Guide them with your heart and know you did the best job you could do by being a conscious awake and aware parent.

I grew up as a small child kneeling on the floor each night with my hands folded over my heart saying my good night prayers. My mother taught me to bless everyone I knew including all the people who needed help. "Now I lay me down to sleep, I pray the Lord my soul to keep. If I should die before I wake, I pray the Lord my soul to take. God bless Mommy, Daddy . . ." and the list went on and on. It became a good habit from a very small age. I think as I grew up and wanted God to respond to my prayers I must have really been in a pain. It paid off however because at the age of ten, the Universe definitely started talking to me and hasn't stopped since.

Teach your children the value of prayer or at least connecting to nature, the playground of the Universe. Let these amazing precious flowers see all the various kingdoms of creation that are available for their pleasure. Watch over them for they are here to shift the consciousness of humanity and need your helping hand. If you are a parent or grandparent of small children, at least for a few minutes a day, just sit and be still with them. Even with a small baby just close your eyes while you are holding them and breathe in the love that surrounds that child. As they age and grow, continue to find those moments each day when you share the quiet connection to the divine. Unplug the telephone, turn off the cell phone and turn off the computer and TV. Create a place of quiet silence that can nurture the continuation of the child's connection to the divine.

I feel these new children of love are the teachers and healers of humanity that often feels is falling apart. What is falling apart is the connection to the lost art of loving and we need their help. These innocent souls are birthed at a time of the great shift of the ages.

They bring in with them a huge field of light and intelligence. They are extremely wise.

As they age, you can learn from them. Pay attention when they want to show or tell you something even if it is their small hand reaching up for the unseen world they are still so sweetly connected to. These are independent powerful souls. Just look into their eyes and you can see the beauty and innocence humankind has somehow forgotten. They are here as we are to remember love. You have the ability as the first authority in the physical world to not only protect this child but to continually strengthen the heart string of spiritual connection to the vibrational state of all that is love everywhere. We are the guardians of their souls. The time will come as they age to carry the torch of divine love and light the way to a better world.

Aging with Grace

Every time I open a magazine or watch a commercial there is something that is related to staying young. If I use certain toothpaste my teeth with look brighter and whiter.

Of course I will attract anyone I want with that smile! If men use a certain pill they can have a renewal of their sex life. I love the disclaimer however that says if you have an erection that lasts for more than four hours or is painful you should go to the emergency room. The boom is on for testosterone sales, plastic surgery and Botox is the new regime for many women. I live in Southern California and the proximity to Hollywood has far reaching effects, but it almost feels like if you look your age you are burnt toast. I do admit I have my face creams, and I am very guilty of the desire to look good. It always surprises me when I see someone I haven't seen in a bit and the first thing they say is you look good. Although I appreciate the compliment, I often wonder if they care how I really am. What has happened to, "How are you?" Are we so programmed into the outer image that we forget to honor the beauty of someones heart? Beyond that, how do we age gracefully not only as women but as men as well?

In the quest for outer beauty there is a continual race and attempt to look perfect.

Hopefully you know that is never going to happen. This is also what the billion dollar beauty business counts on; you trying to make up the difference of what you are told is wrong with you. Since the beginning of time we have tried to make our lives better and that is admirable. There was also a time when we honored our elders as teachers of wisdom. The wrinkles on the faces told us of a journey of experience that stored many emotions. We learned from these elders. Sadly I feel we no longer honor the journey of aging as part of loving ourselves. We feel it is a curse.

Perfection only exists in the state of divine harmony with the soul. Have you ever watched someone meditate and seen the light radiating around their body? Have you seen how rested and peaceful they are when they are done? Have you ever looked into the eyes of a wise old woman and see how those eyes sparkle with such joy? When you look in the mirror every day and see your reflection what do you see? Are you looking at what is wrong or what is right? Our eyes often trick us into blocking the true light of our soul and listing every single thing that we perceive is wrong with our physical body. We judge by what we see rather by what we feel. Somehow along the way we cut the heart string that connects one heart and soul to each other. Have we forgotten that aging is a graceful part of the journey of life? Aging gracefully is walking the path of a spiritual seeker.

How you embrace it on an individual level is private and personal and depends on how you view the elders in your world today. Embracing aging is not giving up.

We live in such a youth oriented society that we have forgotten a heart loved based society. In the native American tradition that I was exposed to while living in Sedona, Arizona it was considered a blessing to have an elder come down from the mesas where they lived to share their sacred wisdom. I felt so blessed when an elder came from the Hopi Tribe to teach a group of clients I had on a retreat in Sedona. We listened carefully.

We didn't question anything and even in those amazing quiet times we felt like the eagle whose feathers he blessed us with. At the end of the day, we sat around his feet as he shared the stories of his tribe and his life. The pride he felt in his tribe's connection and honoring the Earth was like a ribbon he wove around each one of us. Our lives changed because of the time we sat there listening into the late hours of the night. The chanting, the rituals and all he shared he gave so generously with a little gleam in his eyes. We could have sat there for weeks and were sad when it was time for him to go.

I was told that in the tribes of the Mesa, when a woman turned fifty years old there was a ceremony honoring her aging transition. She was now a wise woman of the tribe. I often wonder how many women and men on this earth feel that when they reach the age of fifty. Are they honored for their wisdom? Once we retire from the world of work do we feel we have value? As younger people, how often do they go to the elders? Can we learn from them? Or do we push wisdom aside in that eternal quest for youth and forget that all has divine purpose?

Aging gracefully starts with a state of mind and your personal attitude. The soul never ages. The high holy heart, the heart that is sacred never ages. The world of the physical world may fail us and we may fail it but the world of spirit and your soul never does. I do not feel that aging gracefully means giving in or giving up. It is accepting your life as a continual vehicle for growth and evolution no matter how old you are. In returning to the lost art of loving always remember you are eternally young in the world of light and love.

After my older sister died, she came to visit me in a few dreams. She always looked so radiant and light and young. Her spirit was youthful instead of ill and heavy. I feel she was showing me that after her death and her physical body failing her, she was indeed reborn into her light body. She was free vibrant and content. We do not need to die to be young in our heart and spirit in this life. The Age of Ascension is an age of adjusting to what many call the light body. This body is the emanation of your soul that surrounds and protects you at all times. You have the ability while you are alive no matter how young or old to connect with this light body now. A certain mystical event occurs when you feel you are illuminated. You feel happy healthy and energized. You feel young.

We pay so much attention to the date stamped on our driver's license as a reminder of how we are supposed to feel. When you are illuminated from within, it affects your outer vitality and also your viewpoint of life. Haven't you ever met someone who was young who acted old and vice versa? It had nothing to do with their birth date. Haven't you held a baby in your arms and felt "wow what a wise old soul." How do you know this?

Your true intuitive connection to these people, young or old comes from the knowing of your higher self which is your soul.

The greatest gift you have ever been given is the gift of life. It is an honor to be alive.

The human body has often been called the temple for the soul because it holds the force field of your divine intention to live once again. As you age and actually before you start to age that temple says one thing. Honor me.

One of the lessons I learned about having an almost fatal heart attack was never to take my health for granted. My husband is the king of supplements and probably is the poster child for anti-aging methods. He has been a bodybuilder for over sixty years. He told me that when he was younger, he did it for his ego and looks. As he got older, he did it for his health because he feels his muscles are his currency. He knows his health is his wealth.

Although the inner connection to the world of loving yourself in your own temple should be first, you cannot deny the fact you live in a physical world. Your body needs attention no matter what age you are. The cells and DNA of your body are all there to support you.

You know if you are not healthy. I know somehow we put our health last but as we age, you have got to put it first. Your spiritual, mental, emotional, and your physical health each need separate attention to keep you as a whole being. Trust that inner physician when you feel something is off. In the age of self-reliance it is up to you to be your best patient always listening to the voice of intuition and reality guiding you.

What you reflect to the world is the light that shines inside. The more you love your life see it as a journey that never ends. The best fountain of youth is to be excited for each new moment every day. When I meditate or sit on a beach and gaze at a sunset, I never feel old. I feel connected to something far greater than I can ever express in words. I am speechless. I am timeless. We will all age it is a fact of life. How you age is up to you. Open your heart and mind to the possibility that you are walking on a rainbow of light that is shifting and moving under your feet. Consider it the moving sidewalk of the Universe. It will carry you along. On each step of the journey, you gain insights and wisdom that at some point you can share with others. Prana is energy. It is in the air you breathe. It is the life force that gives substance to the soul. Close your eyes and breathe in the light of awareness all around you. You are not aging. You are evolving!

Parenting the Elders

My mother told me once that she didn't ever want to live in a retirement home environment. I asked her why and she said "because I don't want to be with all those old people." She was 83 years old and living in a condo with my father near my older sister in upstate New York. She was not well. In fact, she was at the end of her life. As a young child, my parents had always had a parent living with them. My father's father lived with us until he died and then my mother's mother came to live with us afterward.

He was Hungarian and a very elegant European gentleman. He lived in Paris at the turn of the century and always came to dinner in a suit. My grandmother was an amazing cook and I learned how to make homemade pies from her even though she had no recipes. She measured with her hands. She loved the Boston Red Sox and was glued to the TV during the World Series. If you wanted to watch with her, you had to be quiet.

In retrospect, I wish now I had spent more time with my grandparents because I could have learned so much from them. In recent years, I have spent time retracing our heritage and did find many records when they were much younger. In my mind I followed their footsteps as they walked through life with births marriages and deaths. I believe I somehow inherited some of their traits and hopefully I am living honorably for our family's spiritual heritage. Although I was the spiritual rebel in my family, I know I chose to be born in this family so I could find my own spiritual journey. It wasn't always easy and as you know my spiritual sisters are closer to me than my birth family as I really am the odd one out.

In many cultures the elders are honored. They are cared for. Their older years are respected by their children and they have a support system. With the economic challenges many people face today families are merging together to help one another which is amazing. Many grandparents are finding that they are the caregivers for the grandchildren while their children go to work.

The family unit that was once shattered is gathering once again as a core unit to help one another. Our family values are also ascending in this Aquarian Age. You may find that unity of family community in your church temple schools libraries or senior citizen centers. As a seeker of wisdom, do we have a responsibility to nurture the elders?

What are we teaching the younger generation about honoring an older person in a youth oriented society? In your own life is there an elder you can share time and love with?

When you see an elderly person who is struggling with groceries do you help them?

What are you telling the Universe about how you wish to be cherished as you age? Are you the woman or man of wisdom that has something of value to share? A return to the lost art of loving is affecting how we love and nurture our elders. How do you personally view the aging process? Is it the loss of freedom in aging that we fear or that we are closing out our time on the earth?

If you have an elder in your life or feel you are at that stage as well, please start the dialogue with divinity embracing the lost art of loving. Affirm to yourself and the world all you have accomplished. You may be surprised at how long that list is. If you have an elder person in your life ask them to share their accomplishments. You may learn something eternally valuable. We have to remind ourselves that we have chosen a life that is filled with various cycles of birth life and death. How we fill in the blanks of the divine plan within those cycles is our choice. Life does not control you. You control it. Death is not something to dread. When it is your time it is a cycle of another transformation. Then we are re-born as a full spirit once again. It is all part of the journey of evolution into a time where the spirit is seen first as the ageless pure light it truly is.

The Art of Dying

I had attended a women's conference many years ago in Phoenix with my friend Sandee where we signed up for a variety of talks. One of the talks we wanted to hear was by Don Miguel Ruiz the author of *The Four Agreements*. He was sitting on a chair waiting to go in to the conference hall waiting for the previous group to leave. I had a moment to go over and say hello. I really wanted to tell him how much I enjoyed his work. He looked very tired.

His talk inspired me because he shared how he had just had a major heart attack and almost died. He also told the audience that when the first chest pains started he called his loved ones to his side. "Come right away I have something so wonderful to share with you, you must come quickly." He told them he was going to give them the greatest teaching ever. What it was like to die. He wanted his apprentices there so he could report everything that was happening to his body and spirit. It really was a profound story listening to this Toltec teacher who had influenced so many of his apprentices or students. Obviously he didn't die. He was so full of the joy when he believed his heart was calling him home. He then went on to talk about the value of life and death being one journey.

I actually met Don Miguel a number of years later while we were both staying at the same home in Carlsbad, California. I told him how much that story had affected me and sat with him as he added to it. What I realized from that moment on, including the time of my own almost fatal heart attack, was how important it is to embrace the concept of transitioning and transformation. Each day we die a little and are reborn once again. It is the continual cycle of evolution. I asked Don Miguel if he was disappointed that he wasn't able to give the full teaching and really cross over. He told me that he felt that the teaching he gave was more valuable than the actual experience of almost dying. The wisdom was to embrace the cycle of life and death, being born and re-born, even when we do not expect it.

One of my favorite very wise spiritual brothers named Dr. Viktor Beasley called me many years ago very late at night. He had some friends who lived in Phoenix whose father was in the hospital very ill. He asked me if I would be open to talking to the daughter and wife of this man. Although it was after ten o'clock at night, I knew Viktor would never ask me to be of service if it wasn't important. I agreed and waited for their phone call. I started to meditate before their call which I always do before a session and felt like I was walking into a hospital room. I just stayed in that energy and when the call came I knew there was a lot to report.

The wife asked me if her husband was dying. I immediately felt lifted up out of that hospital scene and was standing in a family room in a house. I had a sense like someone was pushing me near a big heavy chair. I heard in my clairaudient state the voice of a man saying "tell her my chair is empty". I described the chair to her and gave her the message from her husband. She told me, "This is his favorite chair." I explained to her that I felt her husband would not sit in that chair again hence the message. He was getting ready to make his transition soon from this life to the next. "I thought so," she said.

The next scene I was immediately back in the hospital room. I have to tell you even after all these years I will never forget what I saw. It changed any feelings I had about death completely. I saw an elderly man in a hospital bed with his eyes closed. His breathing was very shallow. Standing next to his bed on the right hand side was a shimmering light in the outlined form of a man. I felt I was watching the spirit of this man outside of his physical body. I almost felt I should stop 'watching' because what was happening between the man and the spirit seemed so private and personal. Then I heard, "Stay, you must report this."

As I watched I saw and felt that the spirit of this woman's husband was getting ready to cross. His spirit had already detached from the physical form of the elderly gentleman laying in the bed. The spirit of the man who was indeed dying was bowing to the man in the bed. His hands were clasped together in prayer. He went lovingly and gently into each single part of the man's body and thanked it for holding him all those years. He went to the organs bloodstream nervous system eyes hands and head. This spirit honored every unique organ and cell bowing and saying thank you thank you thank you.

At this point the mother and I were both crying because we knew his time was almost over on the Earth. It was a very emotional reading. She said, "Although I will miss him, I can prepare myself that he is not coming home." I said, "You know that the home he is going to now, he will prepare for you one day, right?" We said our goodbyes after she asked a few more practical questions.

The next day the daughter called to say that her father had passed away after midnight and to thank me. I thanked her for allowing me to have permission to watch her father's transition at those last precious moments of life on earth. It is a scene I will never forget and one I have repeated many times to people who have any fear of dying. I was privileged to witness the true letting go ceremony of the spirit with the physical body moments before the true art of dying occurred. The gesture of the spirit towards the body it occupied was the most profound act of love I have ever seen.

When I was being wheeled into the operating room the first time I said to my husband and my older son, "I have no fear of dying and I have no regrets," which really is true.

"I am ready to go home if the Universe is calling me there." My husband looked at me very bewildered when I said this for a number of reasons. He was in shock that I was even having an emergency operation and probably in that moment the thought of being alone again as a widower didn't even register in his reality scale previously. When I came home, I realized that one of the reasons I remained was that I had to be there for him. The mantra for the second operation was a little bit different. I kept telling the nurses before they put me under, "You don't understand. I can't die. I have to be there for my husband. He has no one." I continued to be more concerned about his life than mine which was a good validation in being a committed marriage partner.

There will always be more awareness and more wisdom even on the other side of the veils. I do look forward to the trip one day and just hope the Universe and my body cooperates and I can make a gentle crossing. I would love to just float across while I am meditating but that might be pushing the spiritual envelope a little too far. You just never know do you? Live your life wisely and well each and every day. How you live your life now will affect the life you continue to live in the world of pure spirit. Hopefully for you when divine timing says, "Okay time to go" you will be fully ready.

Many times someone will die in the middle of the night when no one is there. I often feel this happens because the soul can be bound to the earth not by fear of dying but bound by leaving loved ones behind. Wouldn't it be wonderful for the future if a process of dying means surrounded by loving people. They are smiling laughing honoring your life and singing your favorite songs. You float away honoring your body and drift across the world of limitations to the loving embrace of the divine.

Living an Ascended Life

$\mathcal{T}$he biggest catalyst for change on the Earth right now is compassion. I have many statues of Quan Yen, the Goddess of Compassion, around my home. They are a daily reminder that in sharing wisdom I also need to be kind caring and compassionate.

Everyone has their own stories, even stories from past lifetimes. It is where we are today in serving the gift of compassion that heals many hearts that are attached to those old stories. The moment you say, 'I understand', you are showing compassion. The moment you listen to another you are being compassionate. You cannot say you are a spiritual person and be unkind. You cannot say you are living in the Age of Ascension consciously when you are judgmental. You cannot say you are a beacon of love when you gossip.

We are moving from right / wrong polarities of judgment and fear into the unification of a new way of serving love on this earth. It is through this serving of love to your own life that you help a greater cause to re-balance the earth from its extremes. You are not stuck with a divine plan that cannot be adjusted through your freewill choices. You have an opportunity as an ascended soul to move beyond the old paradigms or belief systems that were unhealthy for you. You can embrace not only a new way of thinking but a new way of living.

Those that believe in war as an answer believe humankind is basically evil. They add to the energy of anything that is fear based. It is important to remember that the Universe did not create wars. Mankind did through their freewill choices. Love based thoughts and actions bring more love to us. Fear based thoughts and actions separate us from love and cause even more inner chaos which in turn affects the entire world. You can personally affect that result by taking a look at where you feel you are in conflict with your own life.

Living an ascended life has challenges but they can be overcome. There is a leap of faith moment that shows up in every one's life at some point. I feel it is the soul calling you to return home. This doesn't mean you have to physically die. A part of you in terms of old beliefs and a way of living does die. Through letting go of the old and embracing the new attitude on life, you have transformed.

Spiritual ascension is soul resurrection. You do not have to wait until you die in the body and cross over to ascend. People whom I have met who have had near death experiences have told me that they felt so light and free when they were moving beyond the physical body. If that is the case, can you fully ascend while you are still alive? You can rise up from the heaviness of life while you are still alive. You throw off the old coat of karma that needed balancing in this life. You can let go of how you used to live your life through suffering and live from a place of loving. You can be true to who you are, a divine soul in a physical body that is not perfect. You ascend each day of surrendering to divine will so you can get a glimpse of your future. The form of your future self will be created by defining what works for you not what others think it should be. The game of the higher self is one of receptivity and awareness. The receptivity is your own awareness not only of your cognitive boundaries but the divine intention for you to feel content.

It is often said that we are masters walking on the earth without knowing it. You can become your own master by listening to the song of your own soul. Use your discernment. You probably won't want to be out in groups unless you are able to connect and share from your heart, even if it just a feeling of being glad you showed up. The ascended soul realizes that all souls are equal and men and women are brothers and sisters of the same spiritual family walking a similar journey.

The women's movement started a huge wave of energy toward the future by rebelling against old stereotypes and belief systems. We wanted equal pay for equal jobs. We wanted more than that. We needed and wanted a voice. We wanted to be heard and respected. We went to extremes often to get the point across. I do believe we have made progress in some areas but not all. There is still more work to do. Almost every woman I speak with regarding successful relationships has told me that she feels there is a great bond of friendship and partnership with her partner and she does feel they are equal. She feels respected. Men also have shared with me that their successful relationships are with women who they also feel are their buddy, and their teammate working towards the same goal. They feel appreciated.

A person who is spiritually attuned knows that there is no difference between the sexes in the journey of life. Our souls are equal and indeed our paths are often very similar.

Hopefully in all areas of the world's systems this issue of equality whether gender race or sexual preference specific will be a thing of the past. The more we continue to judge as a society we feed fear. We feed separation and we propel the continuation of chaos and conflict. We have to start somewhere and you already know it has to start with you.

You cannot say you believe in one thing and do another. You will make mistakes. You are not perfect. You will have the opportunity to heal your limited beliefs and the limited beliefs of society. It is no accident your soul chose to be here at a pivotal time in history.

The ascended soul applies discernment and knows what works for them and what does not work for them. Often we think we are present when our mind is wandering all over the place. It is those moments of silence that are needed to connect us to the higher self. It is that one breath of prana that carries the light of joy with us through the days of challenges. We consciously know that we are not better than anyone else. We live a humble life knowing there is always more to look forward to. We are on a quest to be the best we can possibly be that is eternal.

Although you may feel you are a small microcosm of energy on the planet do not think your thoughts are not important in global evolution. You have a great opportunity to affect the entire consciousness of the future. This has been referred to as the collective consciousness that sits at the heart of the Universe. We live in a world of unrealized potential that has so much to offer. You personally have a ladder of light that takes you to a future with a purpose to 'be love'.

You are an emissary of light as an ascended soul this does not mean you will not be tested. In the libraries of heaven, also known as the Akashic Hall of Records, each lifetime you have lived is recorded. It is not judged. It merely is recorded as information.

This information is stored for you to review and you don't need to wait until you die to do this. Consider that you are reading a story about your own life right now. You are either at the beginning middle or towards the end of this story of your present life.

The rest of the pages before you are blank. As an ascended soul, in co-creation with the Universe, you are going to fill in those remaining pages. What will you write? It is filled with fluff and stuff? Do you write in a lot of drama? Are you setting the stage for success where good fortune is available? Start writing about your authentic self and see what shows up on the paper. Take your spiritual journal and write from a heart centered place.

Are you living more in the land of Universal love and respecting your soul? Be honest.

Write down what you would like to manifest. Meditate and pray on this. When the time is right, create an action plan inspired by the Universe. Be motivated by your intuition.

Imagine that you are forming a new identity that is brightly lit from the inside out. Those rays of light like a movie projector put forth a new image on the screen of your life on this Earth. Draw in the possibilities of who you are in the future. Imagine that every single cell in your body is moving light through your hand as you re-write the story of your journey. You are planting seeds in the garden of the Universe that is connected to the heart of all souls and all possibilities. Never give up. May you always have faith in yourself and in the goodness of humanity. Start writing be confident and allow yourself to bloom!

EPILOGUE

Precious Pearls of Wisdom

- ♥ Love simply is.

- ♥ You are whole no matter who you are with.

- ♥ Be the master of your mind and the mistress of your soul.

- ♥ Court yourself first.

- ♥ Have a love affair with you.

- ♥ There is a difference between being smart and being wise.

- ♥ The soul's nature is the ideal nature.

- ♥ Ascension is the advanced state of courting the soul to marry the self.

- ♥ Accept the person the way they are rather than the way you want them to be.

- ♥ Let go of trying to be right all the time. It makes life easier.

- There is a big difference between having sex and making love.

- When is enough enough?

- Each day find time to connect with your soul.

- Life is a journey not a race.

- Honor your body with the Twelve Date Rule.

- Like attracts like in the Universe.

- Feel with your heart and think with your head.

- There is a difference between serving your soul and being selfish.

- Wrap your arms around yourself and get a heart hug every day.

- Remember to breathe.

- Laugh often even at yourself.

- All is in divine order

- Soul chemistry that is birthed out of spiritual friendship is the key to happiness.

- The natural state of the soul is bliss.

- Never wait to say I am sorry.

- Always choose Love.

- Drop the mask, you don't need it.

♥ Authentic friends are the best pearls.

♥ Apologize when needed and ask for forgiveness to heal your heart.

♥ A repeat of old patterns can be a repeat of disappointments.

♥ Always whisper your love to God.

♥ Believe in your ability to call in love.

♥ You shall never be lost if you resonate with your heart of hearts.

Peaceful Prayer for Love

I call upon the power of love to permeate every particle of my being. I am in gratitude for all I have thus far, all I am receiving and all I am about to receive. I welcome love that remains with me throughout the veils of time to nurture and heal all that is void of love. Heavenly Father Divine Mother, dearest Friend, all angels guides and teachers of wisdom I open my mind to the belief that Love is my divine state and so it is now and shall ever be. And so it is.

Pearls to Ponder for Self Processing

Whether you have the actual book in your hand or on your e-reader, use the highlight feature or pen to go back and review what tugs on your heart. Pearls to ponder are created to help you on your inner and outer journey as a guideline to get you started. You may also wish to keep a spiritual journal by your side to write down some thoughts or divinely inspired ideas that are birthed while reading.

If you feel it has any value in doing this with a group of people like a book club or a support group, I encourage one of you to be the guide for the group. Try not to get caught up in the personal stories of others. The intention in the group is to help each other come to a greater place of self realization love and support. The entire group can benefit from this.

These are pearls to ponder, wisdom that is lurking beneath the surface in the wellspring of your soul. Remember to be kind to each other, set some guidelines that work for the group and make it your own personal temple of discovery. As an individual person or a group working to support each other, you can take each chapter one by one and share your thoughts and feelings. Keep your journal close to remind yourself that your soul is always growing and evolving. This is a great opportunity to put those spiritual glasses on.

How wonderful to see your life as a pathway to greater awareness wisdom and happiness.

Enjoy the journey!

1. Do you love yourself? Write down six things you love about you. If you are in a group, share these with the group so you can begin to know each other from a positive viewpoint.

2. What are the words you use to describe love?

3. What are the words you use to describe sharing love with someone else?

4. Are there different kinds of love? List what you think they are.

5. Who do you feel loves you more than you love yourself?

6. List three things you could do each day to love yourself.

7. Every night before you go to sleep, take a moment to dialogue with divinity. Do not ask for anything. Do this for a month and see if your life has changed in any way.

8. Keep a journal of spiritual thoughts that you created. Even one word is a thought.

9. How can you start to view your life from a positive viewpoint?

10. How would you define the word relationship? What does that mean personally to you?

11. If you have had any heartache in any type of past relationship what was that? Do you still hold onto that heartache or are you ready to let it go?

12. Are you telling stories that keep you stuck in your past?

13. How can you bring yourself into the present moment with the gift of awareness from your past?

14. What did you learn about yourself as a result of that relationship?

15. If you could re-write your karmic relationship contract with the Universe, what would you say?

16. Write down what your relationship contract would look like with others, i.e., friends, family, co-workers, neighbors, etc.

17. Can you make a positive loving statement about the wisdom you learned even if the relationship was painful?

18. How do you manifest love in your life every day?

19. If you could change one thing about your relationships no matter who they are with, what would that be?

20. Can you find a solution to challenges in those relationships by doing something differently yourself? What would that be?

21. Affirm each day before you go to sleep all the things that showed love exists in the world for you today. Then thank the Universe for the divine support and be in gratitude for all you have, all you are receiving and all you are about to receive.

Acknowledgements

I would like to thank the entire staff at Christine F. Anderson Publishing and Media for their support and genuine consideration of me, not just an author but as a person with a spiritual mission in life.

I have been inspired by so many teachers and friends over the years that is hard to list all of them. On this side of the veil, I thank Beatrex Quntanna, Barbra Dillinger, the monks at Self Realization Fellowship, Dr. Vrisayda Boggess, Joanne Sterling and Rosemarie Ramirez who always encouraged me.

To my dear spiritual sister Rebecca Toft who had multiple heart surgeries and came back after a near death experience, thank you for encouraging me to write my story. Rebecca died suddenly right before her 70th birthday and I know she is still guiding me. Also on the other side of the veil, I thank Paramahansa Yogananda and all the master teachers, guides, saints and sages who sat with me while I meditated and wrote. To my best friend of 50 years Nancy Cianculli I hope you like this book. I miss you so much and hope you are happy in heaven. To Nancy Anne Tappe I still remember everything I learned from you as a sage of our times in Carlsbad, California. To my older sister Dr. Jeanne Kissner, I know that you no longer feel alone and are wrapped in the arms of eternal love.

⁂ *Acknowledgements* ⁂

It is not my time to cross over. I decided to stay and hopefully pave the way for many to practice the lost art of loving in a new way. To my spiritual brothers and sisters on both sides of the veil, thank you. To Doctor Curtiss Stinis at Scripps Green Hospital in La Jolla, California my heart thanks you for being such a brilliant healer and surgeon.

Thank you always my heart of hearts for continually being the pillow for my soul.

had to let go and have faith.
What if I'm not working hed enough?
That's what I've been told over and over

My thoughts ⇒
impact someone else's reality ?:
Judging :

About the Author

Johanna Carroll since age 10 has had a deep intuitive connection to the Universe. Her life turned itself inside out following a divorce in 1983 when she moved from Connecticut to California after experiencing an epiphany moment on a beach in Mexico. She began to study and develop her natural gifts when this connection to the Divine began to speak to her in a unique and unusual way.

She created the first spiritual networking group in San Diego, Women of the New Age in the early 1990s and hosted a TV cable show by the same name. After leaving her hospital healthcare career, for the last 30 years she devotes her life to her international private practice as a spiritual counselor, author, radio host and metaphysical teacher. She has been featured in 3 TV specials on spirituality in

Canada, Japan and the US. Johanna is included in multiple books as an expert in her field and is a former guest professor of metaphysics at Yavapai College in Sedona, Arizona. Her *Get Psyched!* Intuitive Development Training program has opened many doors to the unknown for people in all walks of life. She offers retreats to sacred sites internationally and has written four books: The Queen Who Lost Her Castle, Dialogue with Divinity, My Greatest Love / My Greatest Sorrow and The Lost Art of Loving.

Johanna additionally is well known for her radio talk show *Dialogue with Divinity* on metaphysical talk radio.com. She also offers webinars and on line courses. She has been an avid tennis player for over 60 years and is a devoted wife to her second husband Floyd and her children Scot and David. She is committed in sharing her wisdom with others to improve their lives and embrace joy as a constant condition!

FIND HER ONLINE AT:

Website: johannacarroll.com
Facebook: facebook.com/johannacarrollauthor/
LinkedIn: linkedin.com/in/johanna-carroll-7820429
Twitter: twitter.com/JohannaCarroll | @JohannaCarroll

36349838R00167

Made in the USA
Middletown, DE
31 October 2016